THE SEA

THOMAS LAWS

Travelling between England and
New Zealand
in 1873 and 1901

Thomas Laws (1840–1934) at the age of fifty seven years.
(Laws Family Collection).

THE SEA-DIARIES OF THOMAS LAWS

Travelling between
England and New Zealand
in 1873 and 1901

Robert Laws ● Joanne Jensen ● Derek Laws

First published 2018

© 2018 R. M. Laws, J. M. Jensen, D. G. Laws *editors*
All rights reserved
Published by Robert M. Laws
laws@bcs.org.uk, rmlaws54@gmail.com
This book is sold on a not-for-profit basis.

Cover: 'The Orient Steam Navigation Company's New Liner *Ormuz*', from The Graphic, 5 March 1887.

Preface

In 2003 I inherited a large collection of papers from my father; he never threw anything away. Among them was a non-descript hardback notebook, very battered and with one cover completely detached. It was a hand-written diary from 1901, and it described a return sea-voyage undertaken by my great-grandfather's brother, Thomas Laws (1840–1934). He had travelled by steamer from New Zealand to visit his birthplace in England.

Tantalisingly, in this diary Thomas quoted a short extract from an earlier diary of 1873, which I did not have. It must have covered his initial emigration to New Zealand. With a view to tracking down the earlier diary I contacted my relative Derek Laws in New Zealand. He, in turn, put me in touch with Joanne Jensen, the great-great-granddaughter of Thomas Laws. It turned out that Joanne had the 1873 diary.

The three of us agreed to publish jointly all the diaries, and the result is the volume you hold before you.

R.M.L.
Cambridge, July 2018

Acknowledgements

We thank the following individuals and institutions for their help, and for permitting the use of their images: John Turner of the Ponteland Local History Society and Clare Stephenson for the images of Ponteland, Tony Hisgett and John Alsop for the train scenes, Reuben Goossens for information about the ships, James Martin for Northumberland information, Darrin Ward for the charts of ships' positions, and David Rumsey for the historical maps.

We acknowledge the following institutions: Alexander Turnbull Library, Auckland Libraries, Auckland Weekly News, Museum of New Zealand, National Library of New Zealand, Parliament of New Zealand, Wellington Independent, City of Fremantle, National Library of Australia, Port Chalmers Regional Museum, State Library of Queensland, State Library of Western Australia, The Graphic, Illustrated London News, Tyne and Wear Archives and Museums, Collectie Roermond Cuypershuis, Brooklyn Museum, Church of Jesus Christ of Latter Day Saints, Library of Congress, Rice University, Smithsonian Institute, U.S. Patent Office, Google Maps, and Wikipedia.

We thank Claire Smith for her valuable help in preparing the text for publication.

Contents

Preface v

Acknowledgements vi

Contents vii

Introduction 1

1. Emigrating from England to New Zealand in 1873 17

2. Travelling from New Zealand to England in 1901 85

3. Visiting Friends and Family in England in 1901 139

4. Returning to New Zealand in 1901 227

5. Poetry 273

Appendix 1: Smallpox and the infant deaths 279

Appendix 2: The ships 283

Appendix 3: Who's who? 287

Introduction

This book contains the personal account of three sea-voyages undertaken by my great-grandfather's brother, Thomas Laws. The first voyage was in 1873 when he and his family emigrated by sailing ship from England to New Zealand. The second and third voyages were in 1901 when he travelled by steamer to visit to his birthplace, Ponteland near Newcastle.

Thomas's description of his 1873 journey is unique; very few accounts were written by steerage class passengers to New Zealand, and none has hitherto been published in full. Thomas states what he sees, and he gives his unvarnished opinions of the scenes he witnesses and the people he meets.

In addition to detailed descriptions of the voyages, the diaries also include reminiscences of Thomas's childhood and a personal picture of life in Britain during the late nineteenth century.

•

Thomas was born in 1840. He went to school until he was fourteen, was an apprenticed woodworker until twenty-one, married at twenty five, had two children[1], emigrated to New Zealand at thirty-three, settled there, and had five more

---

[1] A third child died in infancy.

children. He visited Britain again at the age of sixty-one, and died in New Zealand at the age of ninety-three.

He was the first child in a family of three brothers and four sisters, and was born at Eland Green, just north of Ponteland. His father, Robert Laws, was a gardener and farmer, and his mother was Sarah (née Hobson). He married Mary Ann 'Polly' Newlands in 1865.

Thomas and his family emigrated to New Zealand aboard the sailing ship *Douglas* as part of the Vogel programme of assisted immigration. They thrived in New Zealand, and in due course they had a total of seven children who survived to adulthood. Thomas worked for the New Zealand Railways, and he was also a leading light in the Wesleyan Methodist Church, being one the founders of the church in Napier. In addition, he was a City Councillor for Napier and a Justice of the Peace.

The following description of the couple was made at the time of the foundation of the first meeting of the church in Napier:

> The father was of a strong, almost rugged, character of forthright and independent thought, whilst the mother was a gentle refined soul, who ruled that simple home with a quiet dignity and grace.

After the family had been living in Napier for six years, Thomas's brother, 'Bob' (Robert Christopher Laws), also emigrated there. He travelled aboard the SS *Rakaia* in 1879. The third brother, 'Jack' (John William Laws), and the four sisters, Mary, 'Sallie', Susannah, and 'Lil' remained in England.

INTRODUCTION

Mary did not marry. By the time Thomas visited in 1901, Susannah had become Mrs Coulthard; 'Sallie' had become Mrs Dodds; and 'Lil' had become Mrs Thompson.

The family tree from 1680 is shown in Appendix 3. It is believed that almost everyone in New Zealand with the surname 'Laws' is either descended from Thomas and Robert Christopher or is related to them. Indeed it is probable that everyone in Britain with that surname is also related.

•

Economic factors persuaded many people to emigrate from Victorian Britain, but this does not seem to have been Thomas's only motivation. He had a good job, and he was wealthy enough to pay his full fare in advance without using the loan schemes that were available. Furthermore, his wife and her family tried to discourage him from going, but he went nevertheless. Something beyond the economic was pressing him. Although Thomas did not write much about his motivation, an understanding of it can be found through his diaries.

Thomas did not leave a chronological account of his formative years. Nevertheless chapter two, which was written while he was visiting his birthplace in 1901, includes many reminiscences of his early life. As he walks through the places where he had spent his childhood, memories are rekindled and noted down. When these are pieced together, and combined with government records, a full description of his rather unusual childhood emerges. From this, it possible to understand what his inner motivation might have been.

Thomas was his parents' first child, but he was not brought up by them. At the age of twenty-one months he was passed to his great aunt, Mrs Yeaman (Sarah Yeaman née Laws). She was Thomas's father's father's sister. He remained in her care until adulthood.

There were two events that seem to have prompted this informal adoption: first, his mother gave birth to a second baby[2]; second, ten days later, William Yeaman (Mrs Yeaman's husband) died suddenly of a heart attack.[3] Thomas was passed to Mrs Yeaman's care about one month after these two events.[4] Perhaps this was done to alleviate Mrs Yeaman's grief, and possibly also because the new baby was a weak child needing special care. The child died a few years later.

Mrs Yeaman was the owner and innkeeper of the Seven Stars in Ponteland, and that is where she lived and where Thomas grew up. She was fifty-one years old, and she had already adopted four orphaned nieces when Thomas came to her. She had no children of her own and she did not remarry.

Although Thomas was raised by Mrs Yeaman, he would also have seen his parents bringing up his brothers and sisters at their own home at nearby Eland Green. This situation is likely to have had a profound effect on him.

Thomas was 'led to the saviour' at the age of twenty years, and he remained a deeply committed Wesleyan Methodist for the rest of his life. His guiding light was James

---

[2] The baby was born on 3 June, 1842.

[3] William Yeaman died on 13 June, 1842.

[4] Thomas was 'adopted' in July, 1842.

INTRODUCTION

Stobert, the charismatic Methodist leader. James was fifteen years his senior. Thomas says of him: "from my childhood, he had been my spiritual guide, philosopher and friend."

Thomas attended school in Ponteland until he was fourteen years old. After that, he was apprenticed for seven years to a local woodworker at Kenton Bank Foot, which is about three miles south east of Ponteland. After finishing his apprenticeship, he worked first at St. Peter's Shipbuilding Yard in Newcastle-upon-Tyne, then at Elswick Ordnance works, and finally at the shipyards in Stockton-on-Tees.

Thomas became increasingly dissatisfied with life in England, and he developed a strong desire to emigrate. His primary goal in 1873 was to leave England rather than to go particularly to New Zealand: he had, at first, planned to go to South Africa. The strength of the urge that drove him is revealed by his willingness to emigrate alone if his wife and children would not come with him.

In the 1873 diary, Thomas devotes only a few words to expressing his feelings on departure: 'I went to Newcastle, where I joined Mrs. Laws and the children, and said goodbye to my friends'. This is a remarkably bland statement considering that he is leaving probably for ever. He seems to have experienced almost no emotional reaction at all; he does not mention parting from his parents or from Mrs Yeaman.

His behaviour is completely different when he leaves England in 1901 following his three-month visit. This time he is completely taken aback by the strength of his emotional reaction. A deep sense of loss wells up in him during the last few days, and he expresses regret, not only at having ever left

Tyneside in the first place, but also at having returned and thereby having stirred up those long hidden painful feelings.

One final piece of the puzzle of Thomas's personality is found in his relation to figures of authority and leadership. He expects the highest standards from such people, and he does not mince his words when he feels that those in a position of power have failed to live up to their responsibilities towards the weak. He greatly values respect in human relationships, particularly when people are drawn from different strata of society. For example, he expresses particular pleasure when he observes Sir William Stephenson take his stand next to the scavenger[5], Mr. Walton, in the chapel. On the other hand, in Naples he is appalled by the passivity of the church and its apparent inability to help the poor to raise themselves.

Thomas himself frequently adopts the role of a caring, fatherly, reliable, authority-figure; people can look to him for help and guidance. In a sense, he gives to the world the father that he somewhat lacked during his own childhood.

Thomas's unusual upbringing might have led, at least in part, to his inner need to leave his homeland and take himself off to the far side of the world. Nevertheless it is clear that the overall result of his upbringing was the development of a profoundly good and upright man who contributed very positively to the development of an orderly and caring society in New Zealand.

---

[5] A 'scavenger' made his meagre living by searching for lumps of unburnt coal in the ash collected from local houses.

INTRODUCTION

•

Although there are other diaries of steerage class voyages to New Zealand (for example, Donaldson[6] and Teara[7]) none of them has hitherto been published in full. However, Pennington[8] and McNeill[9] present diaries of passengers to *Australia*. Two books that include diary extracts are Haines[10] and Woolcock[11].

An excellent overall description of the emigration journey to New Zealand in the period 1870–1885 is given by Hastings[12], and for a detailed view of what it was like to be a

---

[6] Index of first-hand shipboard accounts of voyages to New Zealand from 1840–1900, Marsha Penelope Donaldson, National Library of New Zealand, item number MS-Group-1944, item 22620399.

[7] The Encyclopaedia of New Zealand https://teara.govt.nz/

[8] Peter Pennington, William Wood's Diary, Ardnamona Publishers, 2002, ISBN 0-9542057-0-7.

[9] Carol McNeill, Round the World Flying, Fife Publicity, 2008, ISBN 978-0-9534686-2-1.

[10] Robin Haines, Life and Death in the Age of Sail: the Passage to Australia, National Maritime Museum, 2003, ISBN 0-948065-70-2.

[11] Helen R. Woolcock, Rights of Passage: Emigration to Australia in the Nineteenth Century, Tavistock Publications, 1986, ISBN 0-422-60240-X.

[12] David Hastings, Over the mountains of the Sea: Life on the Migrant Ships 1870–1885, Auckland University Press, 2006, ISBN 1-86940-375-4.

member of the crew of a square-rigged sailing ship, the reader can do no better than the classic by Newby.[13]

•

This book contains Thomas's complete text and three appendices. The first chapter deals with the outward emigration voyage in 1873. Twenty eight years then elapse before the story is resumed. Chapters two, three, and four comprise one continuous narrative covering Thomas's voyage back to England, his travels within Britain, and his subsequent return to New Zealand. In the fifth chapter Thomas presents his selection of poetry.

The first appendix contains newspaper cuttings relating to the smallpox outbreak on the *Douglas*, the second gives technical details of the ships, and the third explains something of the family tree.

•

Chapter one describes the voyage on the *Douglas* to New Zealand in June–September 1873. Thomas travelled with his wife ('Polly') and their two children, Charles Henry ('Charlie') aged six years, and Frederick Arthur ('Freddie') aged two years. Thomas was named on the passenger list[14] as 'cartwright'. Once the vessel had left the coast they did not see land until they reached New Zealand three and a half months later. Their course took them south through the Atlantic Ocean, almost reaching Brazil, and then east in the

---

[13] Eric Newby, the Last Grain Race, 1956, ISBN 978-0007597833

[14] Archives of the Church of Jesus Christ of Latter Day Saints.

Southern Ocean, passing the Cape of Good Hope and eventually reaching New Zealand.

Thomas's writing shows in vivid detail the difficult conditions under which the immigrants lived. There was almost no privacy; food was scarce and sometimes inedible; the air below decks was stagnant; rats and disease were rife; six children died during the voyage.

The official report on the voyage of the *Douglas* stated that many of the passengers has brought drink with them and that most of the single men had smuggled revolvers aboard, despite both of these being prohibited.[15] It was recommended that the passengers' luggage should in future be searched more thoroughly. The report also suggested that immigrants should be prevented from taking weighing scales aboard 'in order to prevent unpleasantness'. Perhaps this was a direct result of Thomas's complaints about the short rations.

At Wellington, the passengers were quarantined for a time (on Somes Island) because there had been cases of smallpox, bubonic plague, and scarlet fever during the voyage. After the passengers has disembarked, all the interior structures of the immigrant compartments of the ship were removed and burned. After a final medical inspection, the passengers were transported from Wellington to Napier aboard the Government paddle steamer *Luna*.

---

[15] Immigration to New Zealand [Letters to the Agent-General, Transmitting Reports on Immigrant Ships] presented to both Houses of the General Assembly by command of His Excellency, 1874.

Upon disembarking in Napier, Thomas found that he had left his coat and some important papers behind on the *Luna*, which had by then sailed. He also learned that Mr Hebden, who he had thought was going to employ him, had gone out of business. These two disappointments were, however, balanced by a happy coincidence: aboard the *Luna*, Thomas had met Rev. William Morley[16], who was travelling to Napier to assess whether the Methodist Church should establish itself there. In due course Thomas became instrumental in this work.

•

In 1901, after twenty eight years in New Zealand, Thomas took the decision to visit England on his own. Chapter two describes that voyage. He travelled by train from Napier to Wellington, then aboard the SS *Warrimoo* to Sydney, and then on the RMS *Ormuz* to London.

In December 1900 the *Ormuz* had suffered a serious collision with another vessel and had not been seaworthy again until April 1901. Thomas joined her on 10 June 1901 for what was her first major voyage after the repairs. The *Ormuz* was claimed to be the fastest ship in the world.

In those days, steamers could not carry enough coal for the whole journey so they called for refuelling at various ports along the route. Thomas describes these coaling

---

[16] See 'William Morley, 1842–1926: a statesman of God among Australasian Methodists: his work in New Zealand', by Bernard Gadd. Proceedings of the Wesley Historical Society (New Zealand) vol. 20, nos. 1 and 2, March 1964.

operations in some detail. The ships also carried sails because the long run from Fremantle to Colombo was beyond the outermost limit of their steaming range.

The voyage from Wellington to London involved calling at Sydney, Melbourne, Adelaide, Fremantle, Colombo, Suez, Port Said, Naples, Marseilles, Gibraltar, Plymouth, and London. Thomas wrote detailed descriptions of Colombo (seven pages), the Suez Canal (four pages), and Naples seen from the sea (three pages); the passengers were not allowed to disembark at Naples because of outbreaks of bubonic plague and smallpox aboard the *Ormuz*.

•

Chapter three describes Thomas's time in Britain in 1901. He travelled north by train from Tilbury to Ponteland, near Newcastle, the place where he had been born and brought up. He stayed in the north east for nearly three months visiting his friends and relations.

Thomas describes many people, but there are three in particular whom he writes about at length and with great warmth. They are his brother John William 'Jack' Laws and his friends James Stobert and John Jameson. These men clearly had a formative effect on Thomas's personality.

This chapter is important not only because of its descriptions of life in late Victorian Britain, but also because Thomas reveals the story of his early life.

•

Chapter four describes Thomas's return voyage to New Zealand. He travelled by train to Tilbury, then on the

RMS *Ortona* to Sydney, then on the SS *Talune* to Wellington, and finally by train to Napier.

He visited Naples and Pompeii during his return trip, and there are nine pages devoted to descriptions of them. He was very impressed by what he saw, but he was rather shocked by the art that he found in Pompeii, which he had not visited on the earlier journey. For once, he could not bring himself to record what he actually saw but remarks only that 'Some of the paintings cannot be described, but they testify to the low state of morals then existing'.

Thomas visited Colombo for the second time and wrote a further four pages about it including a description of a prisoner-of-war camp for Boers captured during the war in South Africa. Thomas and his brother Jack held completely opposing views about the justness of Britain's position during that conflict. Thomas supported the British government position, but Jack viewed the British as the aggressors.

The next port of call was Fremantle. Thomas's diary reveals that the rules for importing non-native species into New Zealand were somewhat less developed in 1901 than they are today:

> Mr. Edgar Newlands gave me two curious plants known as Stag's horns – a parasite that grows on trees in the Australian bush – I hope to get them safely to New Zealand.

When he arrived within sight of Cape Farewell, Thomas seems to have found the scene rather less uplifting than on his first arrival there. The 1901 diary closes with an impression of tiredness and disappointment that contrasts with his vigour and optimism of 1873.

●

Thomas ended his diaries by quoting some poetry, of which a selection is presented in chapter five of this book. These poems are quoted here as Thomas wrote them down; the text might differ from the official versions.

●

Thomas copied out his diaries in about 1931, and these copies have been used as source material in this book. As he copied, Thomas sometimes added explanatory notes and comments about events that had happened in the meantime, and these have been retained. Thomas's diaries for the period between the end of chapter one and the start of chapter two do exist, but they are not included in this book.

Thomas's words have been left largely unaltered, including much of the punctuation. He used commas more frequently than would be considered usual today, but this was typical of nineteenth century style. Furthermore Thomas was accustomed to writing sermons, which were intended to be read aloud, and he uses commas to denote pauses, not simply to clarify the meaning. This style has been left unaltered except where it makes the text difficult to read. The use of italics and square brackets is entirely editorial.

The formats used for dates and ships' positions have been made uniform and they follow the forms most frequently used by Thomas.

Almost all of the images reproduced in this book are out of copyright by virtue of the passage of time since their date of creation or the date of death of the artist. The world maps are individually attributed to google as required by their 'fair use' licence. A few images are reproduced under a Creative Commons licence and are labelled as such. Some images have been supplied specifically for publication in this book, and these are individually acknowledged in their captions.

R.M.L.

Cambridge, July 2018

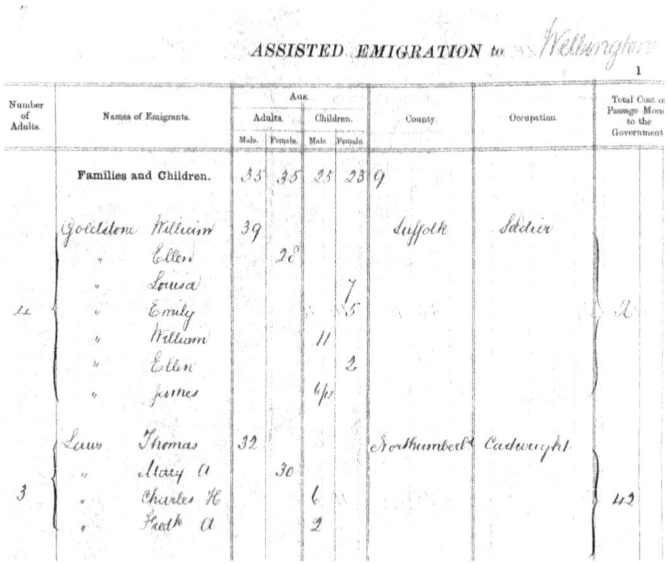

Figure 1 Thomas is shown on the passenger list as a cartwright from Northumberland. (familysearch.org at the Church of Jesus Christ of Latter Day Saints).

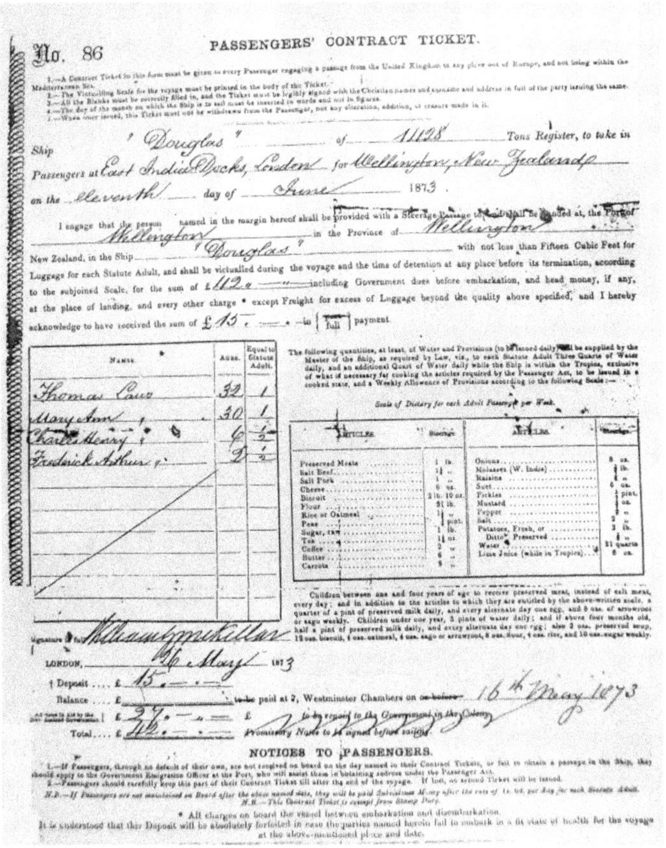

No. 86 PASSENGERS' CONTRACT TICKET.

Ship 'Douglas' of 1128 Tons Register, to take in Passengers at East India Docks, London for Wellington, New Zealand on the eleventh day of June 1873.

I engage that the person named in the margin hereof shall be provided with a Steerage Passage to, and shall be landed at, the Port of Wellington in the Province of Wellington New Zealand, in the Ship 'Douglas' with not less than Fifteen Cubic Feet for Luggage for each Statute Adult, and shall be victualled during the voyage and the time of detention at any place before its termination, according to the subjoined Scale, for the sum of £112 including Government dues before embarkation, and head money, if any, at the place of landing, and every other charge * except Freight for excess of Luggage beyond the quality above specified, and I hereby acknowledge to have received the sum of £15 in full payment.

Names	Ages	Equal to Statute Adult
Thomas Laws	32	1
Mary Ann	30	1
Charles Henry	6	½
Frederick Arthur	2	½

The following quantities, at least, of Water and Provisions (to be issued daily) will be supplied by the Master of the Ship, as required by Law, viz., to each Statute Adult Three Quarts of Water daily, and an additional Quart of Water daily while the Ship is within the Tropics, exclusive of what is necessary for cooking the articles required by the Passenger Act, to be issued in a cooked state, and a Weekly Allowance of Provisions according to the following Scale:—

Scale of Dietary for each Adult Passenger per Week.

Articles	Steerage	Articles	Steerage
Preserved Meats	1 lb.	Onions	8 oz.
Salt Beef	1¼ "	Molasses (W. India)	½ lb.
Salt Pork	1 "	Raisins	½ "
Cheese	6 oz.	Suet	6 oz.
Biscuit	2 lb. 10 oz.	Pickles	¼ pint.
Flour	3½ lb.	Mustard	½ oz.
Rice or Oatmeal	1½ "	Pepper	½ "
Peas	½ pint.	Salt	2 "
Sugar, raw	1 lb.	Potatoes, Fresh, or	2 lb.
Tea	1½ oz.	Ditto Preserved	½ "
Coffee	2 "	Water	21 quarts
Butter	6 "	Lime Juice (while in Tropics)	6 oz.
Carrots	8 "		

Children between one and four years of age to receive preserved meat, instead of salt meat, every day; and in addition to the articles to which they are entitled by the above-written scale, a quarter of a pint of preserved milk daily, and every alternate day one egg, and 8 ozs. of arrowroot or sago weekly. Children under one year, 3 pints of water daily; and if above four months old, half a pint of preserved milk daily, and every alternate day one egg; also 3 ozs. preserved soup, 12 ozs. biscuit, 4 ozs. oatmeal, 4 ozs. sago or arrowroot, 8 ozs. flour, 4 ozs. rice, and 10 ozs. sugar weekly.

Signature in full William McKellar

LONDON, 16 May 1873

† Deposit £15

Balance .... £ to be paid at 7, Westminster Chambers on 16th May 1873

£27 to be repaid to the Government in the Colony

Total .... £42 Promissory Note to be signed before sailing.

NOTICES TO PASSENGERS.

1.—If Passengers, through no default of their own, are not received on board on the day named in their Contract Tickets, or fail to obtain a passage in the Ship, they should apply to the Government Emigration Officer at the Port, who will assist them in obtaining redress under the Passenger Act.

2.—Passengers should carefully keep this part of their Contract Ticket till after the end of the voyage. If lost, no second Ticket will be issued.

N.B.—This Contract Ticket is exempt from Stamp Duty.

* All charges on board the vessel between embarkation and disembarkation.

It is understood that this Deposit will be absolutely forfeited in case the parties named herein fail to embark in a fit state of health for the voyage at the above-mentioned place and date.

Figure 2 The Laws family's steerage ticket to New Zealand in 1873. (Laws Family Collection).

1. Emigrating from England to New Zealand in 1873

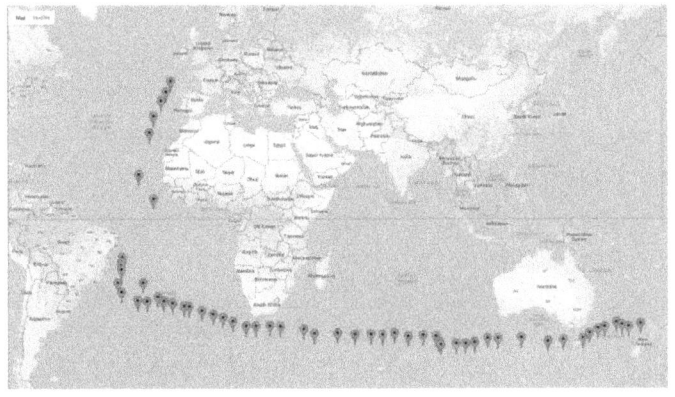

Figure 3 Daily positions of the SS *Douglas* on the voyage from England to New Zealand in 1873. (Courtesy Darrin Ward and Google).

Jan 1ˢᵗ, 1873.

Mr. Jack Newlands[17] is spending a few days with us, he thinks that instead of our going to New Zealand I would do

---

[17] 'Newlands' is Thomas's wife's family surname.

Chapter 1

better by taking a shop in Newcastle market and attending it for a while on Saturdays only.

Jan 7th.

Last night and again tonight Pastor Gordon[18] of Darlington and Mr. Charles Watts[19] of London discussed the subject "Is secularism superior to Christianity." No vote was taken, but judging by the applause Mr. Gordon received, the audience were evidently in his favour.

Jan 12th.

Pastor Gordon lectured in the Circuit on the subject, "Is it reasonable to believe in the existence of God." The building was packed.

Jan 22nd.

The ship *Northfleet*[20], bound for Hobart Town with 400 emigrants on board, was run down off Dungeness, in the English Channel, by a steamer supposed to be of Portuguese nationality. Out of 400 emigrants and a crew of 35, only 95 persons were saved. These were picked up by two or three vessels that were attracted to the spot by the firing of rockets and by the cries of the people on board the sinking vessel.

---

[18] A famous Baptist and former secularist.

[19] A famous secularist and former Methodist.

[20] The *Northfleet* was almost identical to the *Douglas*, on which Thomas was to sail.

The colliding steamer backed out and went off without giving any assistance.

February 1st.

The vessel that collided with the *Northfleet* is the Spanish steamer *Murillo*; the captain, officers and crew will be tried in Spain.

Figure 4 Divers preparing to recover bodies from the wreck of the *Northfleet*. (Illustrated London News, from Wikipedia).

CHAPTER 1

February 26th.

Got a reply from the Agent General of New Zealand giving particulars of Govt. Emigration to that Colony.

March 23rd.

Mr. Cuthbert Bainbridge died today, he was a prominent Newcastle Wesleyan Methodist (and the father of Mr. Edwin Bainbridge who lost his life at the village of Wairoa in NZ, at the time of the Tarawera eruption in June 1887). Deceased leaves a wife and six children.

Note: My diary ends abruptly here, and does not again begin until June 10th, the day we left Newcastle for New Zealand. A few connecting paragraphs may here be given, though culled from memory, and without date.

Up to March 23rd my wife had not given her consent to go with me to New Zealand, and it was understood that I should go alone, and if the country turned out to be what I expected she would come out and bring the children. She very much preferred New Zealand to South Africa. She had a sister living at Blenheim, NZ, two brothers in Victoria, Australia, one at Castlemaine and the other at Melbourne.

The Agent General has informed me that no assisted passages would be given unless the wife accompanied her husband. No doubt these facts greatly influenced my wife's decision, and shortly after my late diary closed, she gave her consent, and I once more approached the Agent General. My application was successful, and we began forthwith to make preparations to leave England.

I continued to work at the shipyard[21] until June 6th, and during my spare hours made six packing cases. Polly did most of the packing, and I helped in the evenings, and this took us from May 19th to 24th.

The bulky pieces of furniture and many smaller articles were sold by Mr. Bradley in his sale rooms in Silver Street on May 26th, and that night my wife and the two boys slept at the house of Mrs. Robinson – Charlie's school mistress – and on the following day they went to Newcastle to spend the interval before sailing with my wife's parents in Cottenham Street. About this date I forwarded my luggage to the railway Station, addressed to "Ship *Douglas*, East India Docks, London", and during the remainder of my time in Stockton I boarded with Mr. and Mrs. Kendal in Stamp Street. Previous to this we had been informed by the Agent General that we were to proceed by the ship *Celestial Queen* to Lyttleton, and would from that port transfer to Napier; later however we were instructed to proceed by the ship *Douglas* to Wellington and thence by boat to Napier.

I continued at my employment until Friday June 6th when I went to Newcastle, where I joined Mrs. Laws and the children, and said goodbye to my friends.

On Sunday June 8th I preached twice at Ponteland. In the congregation were Mr. and Mrs. Bainbridge (see March 23rd). The Bainbridge family were staying at their country house at Dissington, and I was naturally pleased to see them in the congregation, more especially as it was through the

---

[21] This would have been a shipyard at Stockton-on-Tees, where Thomas had moved in 1871.

CHAPTER 1

instrumentality of their son, Master Tom, that I was led to the Saviour in 1860. [22]

I had long been dissatisfied with my position in England, and at this time I was endeavouring to procure a passage to Natal, S. Africa, where an acquaintance of mine was about to proceed, but on carefully weighting the matter the scales turned in favour of New Zealand. How to get out was the crucial question, but after reading a pamphlet by the Rev. Peter Barclay[23], I resolved to apply to the Agent General for an assisted passage, which in due course I obtained.

Myself, wife and two children were reckoned as three adults, the passage money being five pounds per adult, with one pound each added for ship-kit, which comprised bedding, cooking utensils knives, forks, spoons etc., making a total outlay of 18 pounds. Any numbers of pounds less than five would have secured a passage, but for every pound unpaid before sailing, a promissory note for two pounds to be paid in New Zealand, had to be signed, and money had to be paid to a government agent in that country. I am pleased that we were able to pay the full amount, and will be free

---

[22] James Stobert, in 1898, recalled this incident in these words: 'Mr. Bainbridge's attention was drawn to a young man during the Sunday evening service who he thought would be of service to the village. He took the young man by the arm, conducted him into the house, and together they knelt in the kitchen, and there and then Thomas Laws became a useful local preacher, eventually going to New Zealand, where his son is at present a prominent Wesleyan minister.' From the booklet: Ponteland Methodism, published by Ponteland Methodist Church, 2001.

[23] A minister of the Presbyterian Church of New Zealand.

from further liability. We are to sail in the ship *Douglas*, 1,428 tons, Captain John Wilson, from the East India Docks London on June 11th.

Figure 5 Thomas's train was probably pulled by a Stirling Single 4-2-2 of the Great Northern Railway. This new type of locomotive was the fastest in the world at the time. (Photographer: unknown, *circa* 1870, Tony Hisgett Collection, licence CC BY 2.0).

June 10th.

We left Newcastle on June 10th and got to London about 6.30 p.m., the day was fine and the country looked its best.

When nearing London we saw the smouldering ruins of Alexandra Palace, a building recently erected on a grand scale, but which was totally destroyed by fire on the evening of June 9th.

CHAPTER 1

Our first object was to secure lodgings which we obtained in Union Street, and being very tired with our long ride slept sound till morning.

Figure 6 The fire at the Alexandra Palace in 1873 (Illustrated London News, from Wikipedia).

June 11th.

Early this morning we had our luggage taken down to the docks, and paid our dues, and after completing other necessary arrangements, we took the tramway to the city for the double purpose of sightseeing and business. It was now nearly noon, and having to be on board not later than 4 p.m. we had little time at our disposal, and therefore we saw little. We went along Cheapside where we saw the "Royal Exchange" and observed that the text, "The earth is the Lord's, and the fullness thereof", was cut in the stone over the front entrance.

Figure 7 The SS *Douglas*. Thomas and his family sailed on her from London to Wellington. (Photographer: unknown, Alexander Turnbull Library, Wellington, item 1/2-050311-F).

After having purchased a sewing machine, we returned to the docks and went on board. On going down to the married people's compartment, we were greatly disappointed with the arrangements of the berths. We had hoped that each family would have had enclosed berths, or perhaps a small cabin, however plain, and that there would be sufficient light to enable us to read and the women to sew, but it was not so.

The berths were quite open, with the exception of a board 12 inches wide separating the sleepers from the next family on each side of them, we were therefore compelled to dress and undress in our bunks. This lack of privacy was the most objectionable of many objectionable things from which we suffered. The murky light that struggled into the compartment produced a most depressing effect. After having tea on board we turned in for the night.

Chapter 1

June 12th (1st day of the voyage).

At 2.00 a.m. we started on our long voyage by dropping down river as far as Gravesend where we lay all day. Several religious services have been held, and small books and tracts given to us. The ship appears to have taken in a good deal of cargo, about 9.30 we turned in for the night.

June 13th (2nd day).

Lay at Gravesend all day, the time being spent the same as yesterday. Some time was spent in adjusting compasses. The passengers were inspected by the Health Officers. Emigrants gave up their contract tickets, and those who had not paid the regulation fare signed promissory notes for the balance. At 9.30 we retired to our bunk.

June 14th (3rd day).

At 3 a.m. the tugboat *Cambria* of London arrived and took us in tow. The motion of the vessel was so imperceptible that I was not aware she had left her moorings until we were well out to sea. The morning was lovely and several vessels, great and small, were plying in all directions. We kept near the English coast all day, yet could plainly see the land on the French side. We passed Margate, Ramsgate, Dover and Dungeness.

EMIGRATING TO NEW ZEALAND IN 1873

Figure 8 The masts of the *Northfleet* are visible above the waves. (The Graphic, Robert Laws Collection).

It will be remembered that the *Northfleet* was run down by the Spanish steamer *Murillo* on January 22nd *inst*. The masts of the ill-fated steamer were clearly seen as we sailed along.

I was much interested in the appearance of the chalk cliffs, as we passed along the coast, which suggested the idea that it had been Neptune's washing day, and the large white patches were merely the bed sheets hung out to dry. I turned in at about ten o'clock feeling very squeamish.

June 15th (4th day).

Shortly after midnight, feeling very sick, I was obliged to come on deck, and after the usual operation under such circumstances I returned to bed and slept soundly until six o'clock. After breakfast we were inspected by the doctor (Dr. Tuck), and at half past ten we assembled on the poop deck for divine services when prayers were read by the doctor, who has charge of the emigrants it being the captain's duty to look after the ship.

CHAPTER 1

About noon we passed Brighton and New Shoreham. A good deal of hymn singing has been going on all day, and in the evening a prayer meeting was held, at which an address was given by an elderly man named Powell in which he alluded to Popery and Infidelity in such a way as to give great offence to Roman Catholics and others on board.

Note:– Below (Figure 9) is a rough sketch of the married people's compartment showing the lower tier of bunks and the names of the emigrants as far as these could be ascertained by me.

June 16th (5th day).

Beating up the Channel all day against a strong head wind, and making very little progress. The Isle of Wight has been in sight all day, and tonight I went on the forecastle and saw the sun go down, it was really a splendid sight as every wavelet seemed tipped with gold.

June 17th (6th day).

We have been almost becalmed today and our position is really the same as yesterday, the Isle of Wight being again visible nearly the whole day. The weather has been delightful, and as I write scarcely a ripple stirs the surface of the deep.

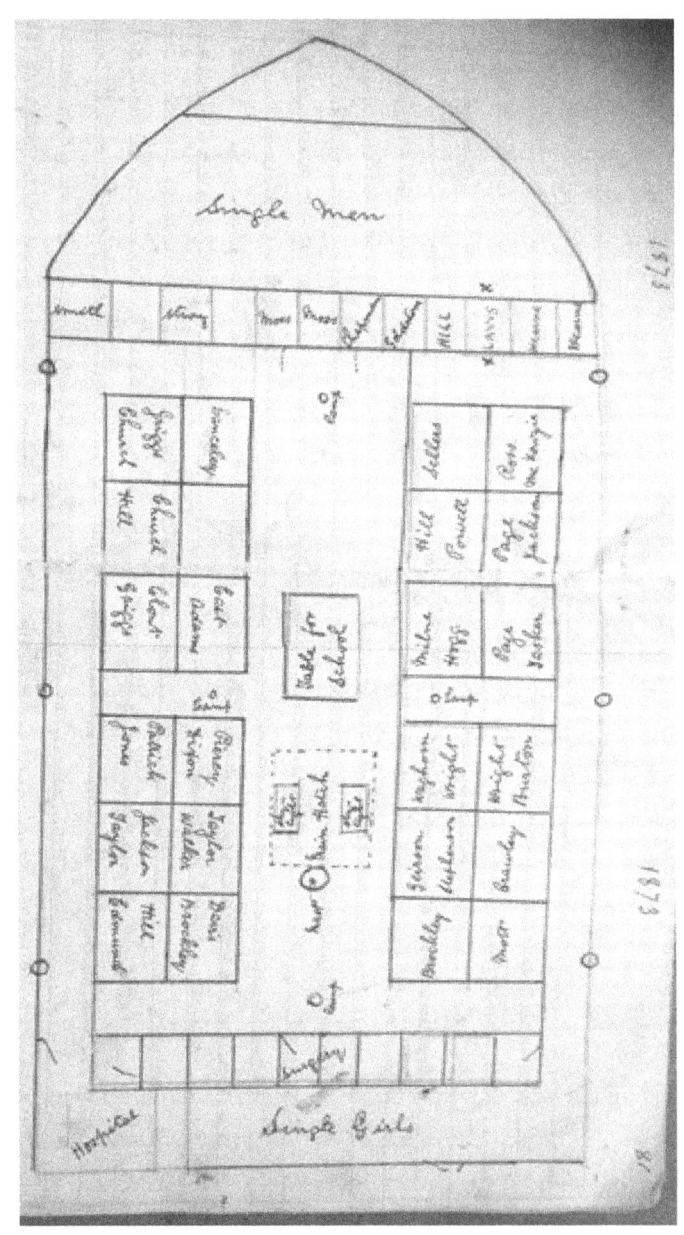

Figure 9 Thomas's sketch of the married people's compartment. (Laws Family Collection).

Chapter 1

June 18th (7th day).

Waterloo Day. There has been a stiff breeze blowing, and we appear to have made satisfactory progress. We passed Portland Point in the night, and today as we hugged the shore we sighted Sidmouth, Budley-Salterton, Exmouth, Dawlish, and Teignmouth. These towns lie low and are surrounded by delightful scenery. The cliffs are not white like those we saw on the coast of Kent, but are of a dull brick red colour. The Channel Pilot left us about noon, we justly regarded him as the connecting link between Old England, and the distant land to which we have turned our faces.

Thursday 19th June (8th day).

During the night we were disturbed by the violence of the gale, and early this morning feeling very sick I was obliged to come on deck and have suffered sea sickness all day, but I have not suffered alone as nearly all on board have been in a similar condition. We have seen no land today and as the position of the ship has not yet been posted, I cannot state even approximately where we are.

Friday June 20th (9th day).

Still sea sick. Saw several shoals of mackeral this morning, they were near the surface of the water which was slightly agitated and much darker in colour over the shoal than elsewhere. My wife fainted this morning and has been in bed all day. Saw land toward evening, supposed to be about Falmouth.

Saturday June 21st (10th day).

The weather has been foggy and damp so that we have scarcely been able to see the length of the ship. In my capacity as "The Captain of The Mess", I have spent a good part of the day in getting provisions from the store. The sailors tell we are nearly out of the Channel.

Sunday June 22nd (11th day).

Inspection immediately after breakfast, and at 10.30, we were mustered on the poop for Divine service: prayers again being read by the doctor. After dinner a large ship crossed our wake hoisting the American flag. We are now entering the Bay of Biscay, where probably owing to increased depth the water is a much deeper blue than any previously seen. I still feel sick, and as neither Polly or the boys have suffered I conclude that I am the only bad sailor in the family.

Monday June 23rd (12th day).

Stiff breeze which has sent us along at a good speed. We are now in the Bay of Biscay. I am told we will cross the Atlantic till we almost reach the coast of South America, then strike eastward and sail in that direction somewhere about 45° of south latitude till after the meridian of the Cape of Good Hope has been passed: the chief officer says it is not unlikely that we may pass within 60 miles of Tasmania,

CHAPTER 1

or that it may even be within sight, and from this point we will cross the Tasman Sea to Cook Straits and thence to Wellington. This appears to be the usual course taken by sailing vessels in order to take advantage of the prevailing winds and currents.

A school of porpoises have been playing around the ship, there must have been several hundreds, perhaps thousands, they advanced about four abreast, the various ranks leaping out of the water with almost military precision.

Tuesday June 24th (13th day).

Weather dull and damp, but this inconvenience has been compensated for by a good breeze which has sent us along at a fair speed. We are still in the Bay of Biscay.

Wednesday June 25th (14th day).

A steady sea has been running today and I am suffering again from *Mal de Mer*. We are still passing through the "Bay" with a fair wind and going at good speed.

Thursday June 26th (15th day).

This is the 8th Anniversary of our wedding day. Who would have then thought that in eight years from that date I, with my wife and two children, would be on our way to New Zealand. Porpoises have again been playing around the ship.

The position of the ship at noon was 43° 18' N, 13° 30' W. Run 210 miles. We are therefore still off the Portuguese coast.

Friday June 27th (16th day).

We have had a good day though not quite equal to yesterday.

Our position at noon was 40° 18' N, 15° 30' W

Saturday June 28th (17th day).

We have had another good run today and at noon were off Cape St. Vincent, our position being 37° 47' N, 17° 20' W. Run 180 miles.

All well and we hope to have got over seasickness.

Sunday June 29th (18 day).

Moderate breeze.
Position 32° 36' N, 20° 20' W. Run not given.

We are now midway between St. Michael and Porto Santo. We saw a few flying fish, one about four inches long and six inches from tip to tip of wings fell on deck, the body resembles a small herring, their flight may be anything from 20 to 30 yards.

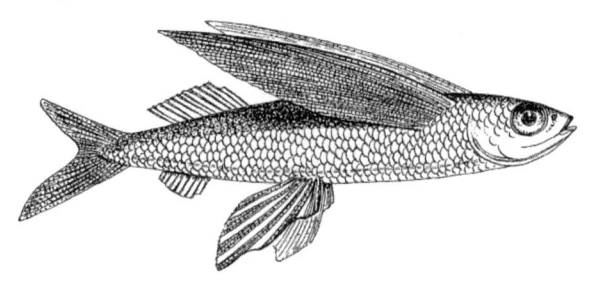

Figure 10 A flying fish. (Pearson Scott Foresman, Wikimedia foundation).

Chapter 1

Monday June 30th (19th day).

We are now off the island of Madeira our position being 33° 00' N, 20° 22' W, having run 162 miles.

As we proceed south we find the weather getting hotter; I have also been struck with the shortening of the days since we left England; it is now only 6.45 p.m. and the sun has set for some time: the twilight also is of very brief duration.

Tuesday July 1st (20th day).

We have had a steady breeze and all is going well. The chief officer informs us that Captain Wilson has given instructions to the effect that the position of the ship is not to be posted in future[24], this is a great disappointment and was to many of us one of the outstanding features of the day.

Wednesday July 2nd (21st day).

The wind still keeps favourable and the weather beautiful, the sun's heat has been tempered by a nice breeze. Saw a few more flying fish from the bow of the ship.

We were off the Canary Islands at noon in 27° 36' N, 22° 45' W.

Took my clarinet on the forecastle this evening and gave the emigrants and sailors a few solos.

---

[24] Perhaps to prevent passengers from demanding lime juice.

Thursday July 3rd (22nd day).

We appeared to have done well today but as we have not got the position of the ship, or the miles run, we don't know exactly where we are. As the wind has been steady for the last few days we believe we are fairly in the SE Trades.

Friday July 4th (23rd day).

Wind strong and favourable. Great dissatisfaction on board by reason of lime-juice not having been served out to emigrants, there is no doubt we are now in the tropics and therefore ought to have received our supply as per contract ticket. Neither have eggs been served out to the children according to dietary scale. Until now these have been supplied, but we are told there are no more.

Saturday July 5th (24th day).

The breeze has moderated and I fear we have made little progress, the captain told us that at noon we were about 50 miles from Cape de Verde islands, though we know not in what direction. We have seen shoals of flying fish and have been greatly interested in watching their movements. The weather is very hot and from appearances we seem to be south of the sun at noon: we have then scarcely any shadow and the little we have is mostly under our feet. Several of the young men are sleeping on the forecastle.

Lime juice served out today.

Chapter 1

Sunday July 6th (25th day).

A light breeze but the weather seems to be hotter than ever. Shortly after dinner, we spotted a large full-rigged ship named the *Calcutta*, outward bound that left England a week before the *Douglas*. I could not discover whither she was bound, but we were all interested in the signaling that went on. Prayer meeting between decks this evening.

Monday July 7th (26th day).

Good breeze: all well on board: weather beautiful; lime juice served out today, dined off salt beef or "mahogany" as the sailors call it.

Our position now is 12° 44' N, 26° 14' W.

Tuesday July 8th (27th day).

Good breeze, dined off salted pork and pea soup. Our[25] first daughter was born today, but unfortunately the baby was stillborn. Nearly becalmed all day, and the heat is unbearable.

Wednesday July 9th (28th day).

We have been becalmed again today and though there has been a nasty swell, the surface of the sea has been as smooth as oil, a fiery sun has been burning upon our heads and as we have had no breeze the heat has been suffocating.

---

[25] That is to say "the ship's first daughter."

Thursday July 10th (29th day).

We have had such showers today as I have never seen before, the rain poured down in torrents.

A small shark apparently about 6 feet long went several times around the ship. One of the sailors baited a large hook with a piece of pork but did not succeed in catching it. Several children are troubled with what appears to be chicken pox and one family has been "ordered" into a temporary hospital on deck.

Friday July 11th (30th day).

We are still becalmed and have again experienced heavy rain and intense heat.

Saturday *July 12th (31st day).*

The wind freshened about teatime yesterday and since then we have done well. One of the sailors caught a fine dolphin which when dying sparkled with the most beautiful colours. Got one of our boxes out of the hold.

Sunday July 13th (32nd day).

Good breeze today. Two fish called by the sailors "Beneta"[26], were caught this morning, they are like the mackeral in appearance but are much richer fish, scores of them have been sporting at the bow of the boat most of the day.

---

[26] Bonito

Chapter 1

An infant died on board this morning and was brought most unwisely into the hospital where my wife and an emigrant named Mrs. Milne were being treated, with the result that both patients were quite upset: Mrs. Milne although exceedingly ill, insisted on being taken to her own berth and this was done. The infant was committed to the deep before sunset, the doctor reading the burial service.

Monday July 14th (33rd day).

We have had a strong head wind today and I fear we have made little progress. I hear that we are about 280 miles north of the equator. My wife is keeping better but needs strengthening food badly.

Tuesday July 15th (34th day).

Strong head wind again today. The cheese served out today was of the filthiest description and smelled most vilely, and on showing it to the doctor, we were ordered to take it back to the steward and on no account were we to eat any more of it.

Wednesday July 16th (35th day).

We are now in the SE Trades and have done well although we have not gone our proper course. Polly recovering slowly.

Thursday July 17th (36th day).

We have had a good breeze today and since noon have run our course, a heavy swell has caused the ship to roll a good deal. Sunset at 6.00 p.m., dark at 6.40 crossed the line at 6 a.m. Someone had stretched a hair across the object glass of a telescope and amused himself by letting others look through, and many were foolish enough to believe they had seen the line. We crossed in longitude 25° 20'. Polly still improving, she was out of bed a little this afternoon.

Friday July 18th (37th day).

I was awoken shortly after midnight by the noise overhead, caused by the sailors shortening sail; the ship was then rolling fearfully, crockery was dancing off the tables, bottles and barrels were rolling about the 'tween decks and things in general were in great confusion. Not being able to sleep I went on deck but the night being dark there was little to see.

For the last few days we have seen large numbers of flying fish, and today the sea seems to swarm with them. Several birds a little larger than the English rook, have been flying about the ship all day, they are black on the wings and speckled on the breast.

Chapter 1

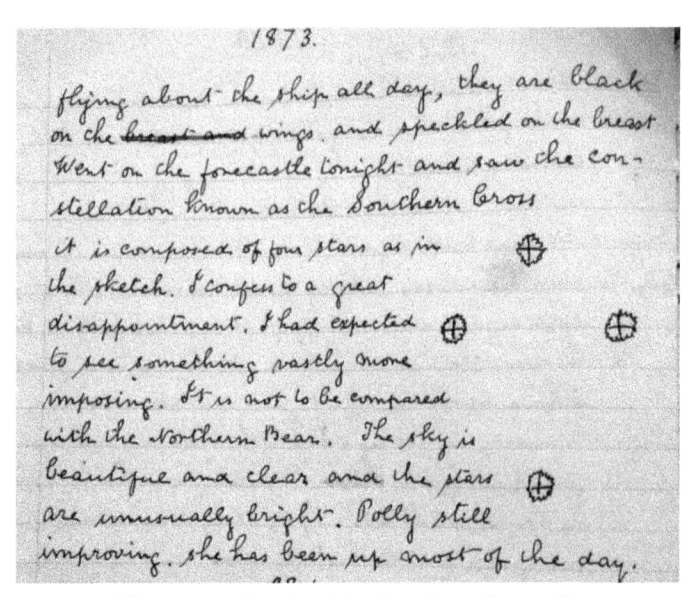

Figure 11 Thomas's sketch of the Southern Cross. (Laws Family Collection).

Went on the forecastle tonight and saw the constellation known as the Southern Cross, it is composed of four stars as in the sketch (Figure 11). I confess to a great disappointment. I had expected to see something vastly more imposing. It is not to be compared with the Northern Bear. The sky is beautiful and clear and the stars are unusually bright. Polly still improving. She has been up most of the day.

Saturday July 19th (38th day).

The breeze has moderated a little and all has gone well on board. I had a splendid bath this evening, the *modus operandi* being simplicity itself. You take your stand in a large tub on deck, one of the emigrants drawing water and another pours it over you until you have had enough. My wife still improving, she went up as far as our berths today.

Sunday July 20th (39th day).

Strong breeze which has sent us spinning along. We are slightly off our course but in other respects everything is satisfactory.

An infant belonging to some people named Mott, died today, it had been subject to convulsion for some time. Several children are unwell with what the doctor says is a mild kind of smallpox but what the mothers on board say is chicken-pox and I pin my faith to the mothers rather than to the doctor. A temporary canvas hospital has been erected on deck for the patients.

Monday July 21st (40th day).

We have had a good breeze which seems to be increasing as I write (8.20 p.m.).

The infant that died yesterday was consigned to the deep this evening, the doctor reading the burial service as before.

It is surprising what little things occasion quarrels on board ship, two men had a set to today as to whose duty it was to fix a table; but when the number of people who are crowded into a small space is remembered, and having dispositions as wide as the poles asunder, such encounters are bound to take place. My wife has left the hospital and will sleep in our own berth tonight.

CHAPTER 1

Tuesday July 22nd (41st day).

Today we have experienced the heaviest sea since we left England, it has repeatedly broken on deck and drenched those who were within its range. I went twice on deck but the night being dark I could see little.

Wednesday July 23rd (42nd day).

Variable winds: and it is reported on board that we have lost the SE trade winds.

Thursday July 24th (43rd day).

We had a good breeze during the early part of the day, but at 1.30 p.m. it fell off and we are now nearly becalmed.

Our position at noon was 18° 22' S, 32° 40' W, which brings us about 150 miles WNW of the island of Trinadad [*sic*] on the coast of Brazil.

Boxes belonging to the emigrants have been bought on deck, and we have taken out a quantity of clothing, and put in that for which we have no further use during the voyage.

There is to be an amateur Christy Minstrel Entertainment this evening.

Friday July 25th (44th day).

During the last 24 hours the breeze seems gradually to have died away, and probably we have not travelled more than 70 miles since noon yesterday.

Our position is 19° 52' S, 33° 00' W, the island of Trinidad being about 150 miles to the SE.

Saturday July 26th (45th day).

Today we have again made little progress, our position at noon being 21° 8' S, 33° 9' W, the island if Trinidad being still the nearest land and lying about 150 miles to the eastward. The sunrise and sunset today were the most beautiful I have ever seen; the clouds assumed the most fantastic shapes, and were tinged with the most brilliant colours, and as I watched the quickly ever-changing scene I was filled with wonder and amazement. I was beginning to think that the glory of the tropical sunsets had been exaggerated, but I think differently now.

Sunday July 27th (46th day).

Heavy rain during the night and early morning. General inspection at 10 a.m. A large shark was near the ship for about an hour this morning, it was supposed to be 18 feet long; it moved in a leisurely manner, with its dorsal fin well out of the water. We have also seen two whales, the first about 8.00 a.m., the second about 9.30, being below I did not see the first; the second appeared to be a black, shapeless mass having neither head or tail: what I saw seemed to be about 20 feet long and resembled a boat turned bottom up; we saw it blow several times throwing up the water to a considerable height.

Our position is 22° 37' S, 33° 04' W, or about the latitude of Rio de Janeiro, the nearest land still being the island of Trinadad.

CHAPTER 1

Monday July 28th (47th day).

We did get a little wind during the night but have been nearly becalmed all day. Three or four Cape pidgeons have been following the ship, they are beautiful birds; head, tail and tips of the wings, black; breast and underneath the body, white; the rest of the bird is speckled; they are webfooted, and dive after any food thrown into the water. Their resemblance to the pidgeon is only seen when they are on the water.

A bird, which the sailors call a molly-hawk, flies about the ship for a couple of hours; it is a large bird, nearly as large as a swan though the neck is shorter. The back and wings are marked with patches of black, the rest of the bird being white.

Position at noon 24° 20' S, 32° 40' W.

Tuesday July 29th (48th day).

A strong NE wind has greatly retarded our progress eastward, but not having the position of the ship we cannot, even approximately, say where we are or whether we have progressed towards our destination.

Wednesday July 30th (49th day).

Stiff breeze. Present position 27° 9' S, 24° 39' W, we are farther west than we ought to be, but our retardation is not so great as we feared. As I write the day is very pleasant; a good breeze is sending us along, about eight or nine knots, the sky is beautiful and clear except for a few fleecy clouds on the horizon, a flock of Cape pidgeons is following in our wake, and a nice mild temperature has given place to the scorching heat of the tropics.

Two more infants died today, belonging to emigrants named Hill and Griggs. I went aft and witnessed their burial, and felt it to be a solemn occasion as their little bodies were committed to the mighty deep.

Thursday July 31st (50th day).

Splendid weather, but the breeze being light we have been moving slowly. The doctor caught a Cape pidgeon, and those who have seen it speak highly of its beauty.

The evening being fine Mr. Wearn and I walked the deck for a long time and had a most interesting conversation on religious subjects. He is a very fine man and is probably "one of the people called" brethren[27].

Position 27° 9' S, 34° 29' W.

Friday August 1st (51st day).

We have been going steadily along at a fair speed. Several Cape pidgeons have been caught today and I have had the opportunity of seeing them at closer range, and the description given them on July 28th is fairly correct. They are caught by two methods. First, by hook and line as in fishing, the hook being baited with a piece of fat pork: this is a very cruel method as the bird must suffer horribly when being drawn on board. The second method, which is more humane

---

[27] That is to say, the Quakers.

Chapter 1

and equally effective, is as follows: a piece of cork is tied to a strong piece of pack thread, this is allowed to fly from the stern of the ship, and as the birds cross and recross in the wake of the vessel their wings become entangled in the thread and they are drawn on board. They always vomit freely when they reach deck and flounder about most helplessly not being able to rise except from the water. This applies to all such sea birds as albatross, molly-hawk, Cape hens and Cape pidgeons. The emigrants are to give another concert tonight. Such amusements break the monotony, and that is all that can be said in their favour.

Our position is now 30° 21' S, 33° 8' W.

Saturday August 2nd (52nd day).

We have had a spanking breeze and made a good run, but the weather has been dull and drizzling. Another whale was seen this morning and also another molly-hawk. About 11 a.m., a large French vessel crossed in our wake, and hoisted her national colours, and the *Douglas* replied by hoisting the British ensign, there was no further signaling except that after a little time, both vessels dipped their ensigns and proceeded on their voyage.

We have seen several birds about the size and colour of the English rook, the body is slender and the wings long and narrow, in fact the bird resembles a huge swallow or rather a huge swift, common enough in England in summer. I could not ascertain the name or other particulars.

A numerous school of porpoises came alongside but were not seen to such advantage as those we saw in the Bay of Biscay on June 23rd.

Sunday August 3rd (53rd day).

Strong quarter breeze and the ship is much "laid up" that we can scarcely walk along the deck. Saw another ship this morning, the vessel seemed to be a full rigged ship going in the same direction as ourselves but we soon left her behind. There was no signaling. I supposed the distances prevented that being done. We have been followed by a large number of Cape pidgeons and Cape hens. The latter is a large black bird measuring seven or eight feet across the wing from tip to tip.

Position 32° 59' S, 26° 46' W.

Monday August 4th (54th day).

Strong breeze and heavy seas; we have rolled about a good deal and things in general have been very unpleasant. Our position now is 33° 20' S, 23° 00' W.

Tuesday August 5th (55th day).

The heavy weather continues and the ship rolls as much as during yesterday; it is also getting much colder and we are discarding our light clothing and are resorting to overcoats and mufflers.

Our position at noon was 32° 59' S, 26° 46' W.

CHAPTER 1

Wednesday August 6th (56th day).

The breeze has moderated and the sea has gone down considerably.

Another infant died this morning, its parents are named Brockley. No wonder so many of these little mites are passing out; there is no proper nourishing food on board for them or for a nursing mother, and these infants cannot struggle against the improper food they get; and all the discomfort and inconvenience of an emigrant ship. The infant that died today is the sixth since we came on board.

Position 31° 49' S, 18° 50' W.

Thursday August 7th (57th day).

Light wind and little progress, but the weather has been beautiful. It is a splendid moonlight night and after the children had gone to bed Polly and I took a long walk on deck.

Friday August 8th (58th day).

A little rain during the night, but the day has been beautiful. We have had a good breeze and our position today is 33° 05' S, 16° 29' W.

Saturday August 9th (59th day).

Good breeze and a capital run.

Position 33° 50' S, 12° 57' W, which is almost the latitude of the Cape of Good Hope. Two or three molly-hawks have been in company with us today.

Mr. and Mrs. Brockley, whose infant died on Wednesday last, have had the gap filled today, by the birth of a son.

Sunday August 10th (60th day).

Good breeze and a very satisfactory run.
Our position is 34° 41' S, 8° 21' W. Run 255 miles.
The nearest land is Tristan de Acuna, which lies about 200 miles to the SW. A great number of Cape pidgeons have been alighting near the ship, and greedily devoured any scraps thrown to them; they seem absolutely without fear.

Monday August 11th (61st day).

A good breeze and a heavy sea. A concert was given by the single men, the principal feature seemed to be the lack of talent displayed by the company.
Position of the ship 34° 51' S, 6° 21' W.

Tuesday August 12th (62nd day).

The ship had been almost under bare poles, and has run 270 miles during the last 24 hours. Our position at noon was 36° 9' S, 1° 11' W, and as I write we will be just about the meridian of Greenwich and have the same time as in England. Napier lies in 175° E and will be twelve hours less twenty minutes ahead both of England and all places on the meridian of Greenwich. Molly-hawks, Cape hens, Cape pidgeons and snow birds, have been following us; the latter is a pretty bird of a light dove colour and fairly sparkles in the sun as they fly.

CHAPTER 1

Position 38° 19' S, 6° 57' E. Nothing else to record.

Wednesday August 13th (63rd day).

Moderate breeze and, in contrast to the ship yesterday, we have now every stitch of canvas set. Our position at noon was 37° 21' S, 3° 12' E. We would therefore pass the meridian of Greenwich yesterday afternoon. Run 230 miles during the last twenty four hours.

Figure 12 Working the sails of a square-rigged ship[28] in rough weather. (Photographer: uncertain, perhaps Alexander Harper Turner, De Maus Collection, Alexander Turnbull Library, item 1/2-014494-G, from Wikipedia).

---

[28] The ship is the *Garthsnaid* photographed in 1920. Whoever took it, must have climbed up the rigging carrying the large glass-plate camera.

Thursday August 14th (64th day).

Weather fine, and a good steady breeze blowing.

Friday August 15th (65th day).

Strong westerly wind that has carried us along splendidly. Five children are now in hospital suffering from scarlet fever – so the doctor says. I caught a Cape pidgeon today by the second method as mentioned on day 51.

Position 39° 22' S, 10° 57' E. Run 207 miles.

Saturday August 16th (66th day).

A very disagreeable day; the wind being very strong, and the rain has been coming down incessantly. Late in the evening we had heavy thunderstorms when every lightening flash illuminated the ship as well as the stormy sea, the thunder pealed as I have seldom heard it.

During the storm we were caught in a squall which carried away the fore top sail, and sent some of the gear down on the deck with great noise. Happily few if any of the emigrants were on the deck at the time and none were hurt. For a short time the wind fairly whistled through the rigging, but the uproar and confusion have now passed away, as though the voice of Omnipotence had once more stilled the contending elements by his Peace.

Our position is 40° 40' S, 16° 15' E. Run 254 miles.

Chapter 1

Sunday August 17th (67th day).

It has rained incessantly all day and consequently few have appeared on deck except those engaged in working the ship. One of the single women had a narrow escape from a severe or possible fatal accident. When the ship was rolling she was unable to keep her feet, and fell from the poop head foremost into the alley-way below. Had the ship gone a little farther over, she would almost undoubtedly have gone overboard. As it is, she has cut her head badly and has been carried down to her berth.

Position of the ship 40° 45' S, 20° 00' E[29]. Run 235 miles.

The Cape of Good Hope lying about 400 miles to the nor west.

Monday August 18th (68th day).

We have had rough day, the wind and sea being much higher than yesterday and few have ventured on deck, the ship's decks have several times been flooded and so have those who would not remain below deck getting water for tea. The vessel was rolling terribly, so much so that it was with difficulty I could get along the deck, and it was impossible to stand still. On going below I found everything in state of confusion; the treacle and sugar had rolled off Goldstone's table into my wife's lap; their tea had upset onto Charlie's; he and Fred were crying and speaking generally things were in a state of chaos.

---

[29] Their position indicates that they now have passed the southernmost point of Africa.

Position 40° 47' S, 25° 30' E. Run 235 miles.

Tuesday August 19th (69th day).

Another rough day. About 5.30 this morning we were struck by a heavy sea that carried away one of the large troughs at which the emigrants did their washing; and lifting the cover of the main hatchway the water poured down between decks, to the discomfort and fear of those whose berths were in the after-part of the compartment. Fortunately our berths lay well forward and we suffered comparatively little inconvenience. The water was knee deep and splashing about in the hospital, quite over the lower tiers of beds, and wetting Mrs. Brockley, who unfortunately occupied one of them. (see August 9th). It took several hours for a gang of men to carry out the water and make the place a little comfortable.

Position 40° 48' S, 29° 47' E. Run 204 miles.

Wednesday August 20th (70th day).

Weather a little better, we have had a fairly good breeze and made a good run.

Position 41° 5' S, 34° 42' E. Run 238 miles.

The nearest land is now Prince Edward's Island.

Thursday August 21st (71st day).

We had a good breeze during the night, but it was much lighter during the forenoon. Went aft this afternoon and caught three Cape pidgeons.

Chapter 1

Position of the ship 41° 36' S, 39° 00' E. Run 205 miles.

Friday August 22nd (72nd day).

This has been a dull damp day, but we have enjoyed a fair wind, which evens matters up. On account of the sickness among the children, the doctor had commanded the married people's compartment to be fumigated: so, shortly after dinner, all had to turn out on deck, notwithstanding the cold and drizzling rain, where we were kept for two hours. As many of the women and children as could crowd into the single girls compartment were allowed to shelter there, but it became so crowded that many were glad to get on deck again, where we stood sheltering as best we might, until it was considered safe to return. I believe that such an experience as we had today, more likely to produce than cure illness. If fumigation was necessary, surely it ought to have been done when the weather was fine.

A large number of birds have been following the ship. Albatross, molly-hawks, snow birds, Cape hens, Cape pidgeons and stormy petrels. We have seen none of the latter since we were off the coast of Portugal.

Position 42° 55' S, 43° 10' E. Run 200 miles.

Saturday August 23th (73rd day).

Another wet, cold, day.

Our position at noon was 42° 53' S, 48° 32' E. Run 248 miles.

The Chief officer says we are now 5700 miles from Cape Farewell at the entrance to Cook Strait, New Zealand.

Sunday August 24th (74th day).

Wind fair, though too little of it: weather fine but cold. Divine service held in the single women's compartment. This morning a large number of black fish were seen at a short distance from the ship, but they were not sufficiently near to examine closely. We dined off Cape pidgeon which was pronounced by all to be excellent. Mr. and Mrs. Wrane and family dined with us.

Position 42° 45' S, 52° 22' E. Run last 24 hours 180 miles.

Monday August 25th (75th day).

The wind has improved since yesterday, but the weather is still cold, and a fairly high sea is running. The 'tween decks at night presents quite a busy appearance. As I write various groups are talking over the affairs of the day. Others are playing draughts, one man of a more practical disposition than his neighbours is making a child's chair out of an empty beef cask the only tool employed being his pocket knife. Some are having supper.

Many of the women are sewing and knitting, small parties of both sexes have grouped themselves around the hanging lamps, seeking for small insects that they have no particular desire to discover, but which are now only too plentiful. During the early part of the voyage this quest, if made at all, was done by stealth; it is now done openly and without shame, for no one can point a finger at his neighbour.

Chapter 1

Tuesday August 26th (76th day).

Wind fair but light and the weather a little warmer than yesterday.

Position 43° 10' S, 59° 16' E. Run 110 miles.

Wednesday August 27th (77th day).

We have had a stiff breeze, and the weather has been as disagreeable as ever. About midnight one of the sails was carried away bringing some heavy tackle down with it.

A similar accident is recorded on August 16th, and happily in neither case was any serious damage done. We have shipped some heavy seas, which as usual have drenched those who were on deck.

Position 43° 15' S, 65° 31' E. Run 290 miles; which so far is a record for the voyage.[30]

Thursday August 28th (78th day).

We had a very strong breeze during the night, the ship rolling so heavily that sleep was out of the question, and all day we have been running under close reefed topsails; the sea has been stormy, and the vessel tumbling about so much that we could hardly stand on deck. After dinner a heavy shower of hail fell, and at 3 p.m. we were caught in a heavy squall

---

[30] The 'day' for a ship sailing east in the Southern Ocean is about 23½ hours. 290 miles compares well with the record of 315 miles in 24 hours set by the *Moshulu* when she won the Last Grain Race in 1939.

when the rain came down in torrents and the wind blew a hurricane: the storm was of brief duration and passed over without doing any damage. These squalls come with amazing suddenness and are seen just before they strike the ship, and so give the officers no time for preparation. The squall today did not last more than fifteen minutes.

Position 43° 22' S, 70° 11' E. Run 220 miles.

Friday August 29th (79th day).

Strong breeze during the last 24 hours. The sea is still running high though not so stormy as yesterday, caught two more Cape pidgeons.

Position 42° 49' S, 74° 49' E. Run 215 miles.

Saturday August 30th (80th day).

Good breeze and comparatively calm sea.

I think we are all about tired of a seafaring life, in which those who have lived on land find so many discomforts. To begin with; the meat is very inferior in quality, and, as bad as it is, we get too little of it: it is always short in weight; when pork it is always so fat that we cannot eat it, and when beef is served out, we get about one third bone weighed in with it.

Our dietary scale has been cut down in other ways. I know that on July 4th we were well within the tropics and lime juice ought to have been served out previous to that date, as a matter of fact I have discovered that we entered the tropics and ought to have had our allowance of lime juice on July 2nd, but we did not receive it until July 7th.

Chapter 1

During the early part of the voyage the cheese served out to the emigrants was pronounced by the doctor to be unfit for consumption, and the eggs for the use of children went rotten, which the steward attributed to the hot weather, the consequence being that neither cheese or eggs have been served out since.

Everything we get in the way of provisions is short; either in weight or measure, and as we are only emigrants, I need hardly add, are deficient in quality and badly cooked. If we complain to the steward we get nothing but abuse and as a rule we get little satisfaction by complaining to the doctor. By small tips I have managed to keep the cooks pretty square and so, compared with others I have little to complain of, but I am disgusted at the bullying, insulting, way they treat most of the emigrants.

Another source of annoyance is the bad language to which we are forced to listen. I refrain from going into details on this subject. I have listened to wicked expressions too often, but for low brutal vulgarity, the immigrants on board the ship *Douglas* take the cake. We hear it wherever we are by day and we hear it by night, there is plenty of it in our compartment and, as we are only separated from the single men's compartment by a thin bulkhead, we hear language at which Satan himself might blush.

Then, as mentioned at the beginning of this log, another source of trouble is the poor light we get between decks, especially at our end of the compartment where we can scarcely see to read or write by night or day. I referred to the great lack of privacy in my log of June 11th and need not again to touch upon the subject here.

Then there are the noises overhead, especially at nights. Right over our berth a condensing engine (Figure 13) is fixed, it is used for the purpose of processing fresh water for the ship's use, and runs night and day. It makes a fearful noise, though we are more accustomed to it now than at the beginning of the voyage. Add to this the noise of the watch on deck as they increase or shorten sail, their shouts, stamping, and throwing things about making sleep impossible. Then there is the rolling and pitching of the vessel with the accompanying of upsetting buckets and plates and dishes tumbling from shelves.

Figure 13 Chaplins' patent sea-water distilling apparatus for sailing vessels, which kept Thomas awake at night.
(Illustrated Catalogue of Chaplins' Patent Steam Engines and Boilers 1883, from Wikipedia).

Chapter 1

Another cause of discomfort is the almost continual sloppy state of the deck, day by day, and many times in the day, one spray after another keeps coming over and the decks are wet almost continuously. During the former part of the voyage we could sit most of the day on deck and often had our dinners there; but that is now out of the question.

The great number of rats on board is another nuisance, for the first few weeks we saw no signs of these vermin, but as the voyage proceeded first one then more made their appearance until now they run about the ship in all directions, even over us as we lie in bed. The other day one of them ran up the clothes of a little girl named Strong, and a day or two after, another ran up the clothes of a woman named Chapman. The pests have gnawed the clothes of some of the emigrants until they are now quite useless. I am glad to say we have not suffered in this respect. No good service would be rendered by adding to the list though this could be easily done.

Position of the ship 43° 44' S, 80° 20' E. Run 260 miles.

Sunday August 31st (81st day).

Good breeze and better weather than yesterday. Inspection this morning at ten, after which divine service was held in the single girls' compartment.

Position at noon 43° 27' S, 86° 6' E. Run 270 miles.

Monday September 1st (82nd day).

Good breeze during the night, but towards morning it went down considerably and has been light all day.

Position 43° 44' S, 91° 00' E. Run 225 miles.

Tuesday September 2nd (83rd day).

Strong head winds, a rough sea, and very unpleasant weather. Nothing of importance to record.
Position 45° 11' S, 92° 11' E. Run 100 miles.

Wednesday September 3rd (84th day).

Strong head wind again today and the ship rolling and pitching at a great rate. I have felt very much off colour, more so than at any time during the voyage, this is probably the result of the rough weather and the rolling and pitching of the ship. I have been obliged to keep myself quiet in bed.

I am told that large birds have been caught by the sailors—a molly-hawk, having a black body and white wings—and a Cape hen which is entirely black. The sailors very kindly brought them down between decks for us to see. They each measured six feet across the wings from tip to tip.

Position 45° 57' S, 93° 2' E. Run 66 miles, which is the worst we have done.

Thursday September 4th (85th day).

The wind got round about 8 p.m. last night and has been favourable, but the ship continues to roll as much as ever. We could hardly sleep a wink last night for the noise caused by the tin plates and other tin utensils first off one table and then off another, and afterwards dancing all sorts of capers at every lurch of the vessel.

CHAPTER 1

Position 45° 43' S, 99° 00' E. Run 199 miles.

Friday September 5th (86th day).

Strong quarter breeze and a heavy sea.

A young man named Griffiths[31] has been put in irons for refusing to pump water for the use of the emigrants. Two more Cape hens have been caught, both were the same size and colour as the one described on Wednesday last.

The ship has been rolling severely all day and tonight I think she is getting worse. I twice slid the full length and completely over the end of the bench on which I had expected to find repose. About ten o'clock when all the married people had retired except a man named Lanceley and myself. The ship was going along comparatively steadily, and availing myself of what I considered a lull in the storm I was leaning against an iron stanchion writing my log. Lanceley was sitting on the deck just in front of his berth having supper with the plate of cold meat on his knee. It was at this moment that the ship began to kick most viciously, and to prevent myself from falling I let fall the log and clasped my arm around the stanchion behind me. But Lanceley, having no such friend at hand, was obliged to submit to the course of events: his plate of meat eluded his grasp and rolled off to various parts of the compartment and Lanceley himself went through some peculiar movements while in a sitting posture sliding about the deck as though following hard after his cold meat and concluding his

---

[31] George Griffiths was an eighteen year old Navvy from Glamorganshire.

gyrations in a spread-eagle fashion at my feet. Mr. Adams's bag of rice came down from the shelf and paid a complementary visit to Mr. Hill's tub of biscuits, and after a short time together, walked or rather slid off in company. A miscellaneous collection of articles were now tripping "the light fantastic toe" with every lurch of the ship.

Figure 14 A 'British Bulldog' revolver current in 1873. Most of the single men had taken revolvers aboard with them. (Smithsonian Institute, from Wikipedia).

How long the entertainment might have lasted had the audience remained as select as at the beginning I don't know, but hearing how fast and furious was the fun we were having, a head was popping out of one berth and then out of another until the performance was becoming too public, so we resolved to adjourn.

A deputation of young men waiting upon the captain this evening to procure the release of Griffiths, but their efforts were unavailing.

Chapter 1

Position of the ship 45° 40' S, 102° 40' E. Run 170 miles.

Saturday September 6th (87nd day).

Good breeze all day.

There is a good deal of unpleasantness going on between the young men and the officers on board. The young men, not being able to secure the release of Griffiths, last night held a meeting and resolved to do no work of any kind until he is set at liberty. This coming to the ears of the captain, the young fellows were ordered to the poop and severally asked whether they were willing to conform to the ship's regulations; some agreed while others declined. This being the case, the mutineers are to receive no more rations until they come to a better state of mind. The messes therefore have been re-arranged and the malcontents put by themselves.

Position 45° 20' S, 106° 10' E. Run 160 miles.

Sunday September 7th (88th day).

We have had another very rough day. Early this morning we were struck by a heavy sea which once more lifted the cover over the main hatch and the water poured down upon us who were in the married people's compartment. Once more I have to be thankful that our berth was well forward, for the water ran aft as on a former occasion leaving our part of the ship comparatively dry, some of the emigrants suffered severely. The water from the flooded end of the compartment was bailed out by the sailors and a few volunteers. Griffiths was set at liberty last night and the young men have all become submissive.

Position 44° 16' S, 111° 20' E. Run 265 miles.

Monday September 8th (89th day).

A good breeze but an unusually high sea, in fact we seem at times to be so engulfed that we cannot see further than the length of the ship in any direction. Poor little Fred and I got a regular sousing this afternoon. Being rather fretful below I took him on deck for a change; we had just seated ourselves on the lee side of the galley when a great sea came over and drenched us thoroughly. A little boy named Goldstone suffered in like manner, and when retelling the news to a group of emigrants, his mother said there wasn't a dry thread on him but what was wet. The same might be said of Fred and me. We are now off the coast of Australia, about 700 miles from Cape Lewin at the south western extremity of that continent.

Position 44° 19' S, 115° 16' E. Run 240 miles.

Tuesday September 9th (90th day).

Good breeze during the last 24 hours, but the ship still rolls too much to be pleasant. Heavy rain fell about 7 p.m.

Position 44° 00' S, 120° 16' E. Run 215 miles.

CHAPTER 1

Wednesday September 10th (91st day).

Strong quarter breeze, resulting in the ship being very much laid up. Went aft and caught two more Cape pidgeons. Heavy rain this evening.
Position 44° 02' S, 124° 25' E. Run 190 miles.

Thursday September 11th (92nd day).

A good breeze and a very quiet sea.
Position 44° 37' S, 128° 57' E. Run 196 miles.
Nothing of much interest to record today.

Friday September 12th (93rd day).

The wind has been very strong and we have shipped some heavy seas. I ought to have stated that during the late heavy weather, ropes have been run to various parts of the deck, in order that we may move easily, and with greater safety get about the ship, these helps to locomotion are available today.

There is a case in hospital which the doctor has declared to be fever, but the emigrants one and all, gravely doubt his diagnosis.
Position 45° 00' S, 134° 50' E. Run 170 miles.

Saturday September 13th (94th day).

The breeze has been light and our run correspondingly short. During the last few days we have been passing through the Great Australian Bight and are now 700 miles distant from Adelaide, the capital of South Australia. Another Cape hen was caught today.

Position 45° 05' S, 134° 50' E. Run 125 miles.

Sunday September 14th (95th day).

Today we have had the roughest sea that we have experienced during the voyage. I have heard about the sea running "mountains high', but I have now witnessed something closely akin to that experience.

At 7.30 am I took some oatmeal to the galley for our porridge and on returning stopped to speak to one of the ship's apprentices and two of the emigrants; while we were chatting a heavy sea rolled in on us. I am told it came in three feet above the bulwarks and the full length of the deck. The apprentice was knocked down and washed into the lee scuppers and to prevent ourselves meeting a similar fate, myself and the other two emigrants ran to the side of the ship and laid hold on the belaying pins, there we stood a considerable time, till in an unlucky moment I was tempted to make for the main hatchway with the intention of gaining the flat portion at the top of the skylight where I hoped to be clear of the water, but just when making the attempt the ship made a sudden and unexpected lurch that caused me to miss the hatchway entirely and drove me to the other side of the deck where the apprentice was still floundering. There I stood hanging on to the belaying pins, now high and dry as the vessel rolled to the weather side and again swept off my feet and thoroughly soused as she rolled to leeward. In due

CHAPTER 1

time however the water got off through the scuppers and its abatement brought us relief.

Figure 15 A square-rigged sailing ship in the Southern Ocean. (Photographer: unknown, National Library of Australia, item PIC/8807/107, from Wikipedia).

A man named Crawley had a worse experience; he was mounting the companion ladder just when the sea struck the ship and the water poured down upon him and, but for the handrails to which he clung, he would undoubtedly have been swept into the married people's, compartment so recently left. When coming out of the door he presented a miserable appearance: the water being cold took away his breath and was dripping from his hair, whiskers and clothes.

We were again struck by a heavy sea about 4 p.m. when the captains of messes were on deck getting hot water for tea: fortunately I was in our compartment at the time and so escaped a second wetting or worse. Several of those on deck were knocked down, some being severely hurt; the hatchway already mentioned was badly damaged, one of lavatories was washed a few yards from its position, the pig house, including its occupants was also moved a considerable distance though fastened to the deck with strong ropes.

Many thought we were going down, women were screaming, children crying and a state of general confusion prevailed. While on the forecastle this afternoon the scene was grand, beyond my pen to describe. I make no profession of judging the height of waves in a storm at sea, but I would estimate the height of those we saw today to be not less than 50 feet or 60 feet.

Position 44° 38' S, 140° 50' E. Run 264 miles.

Monday September 15th (96th day).

The breeze and the sea have gone down considerably. We are now about 80 miles to the south of Tasmania, which is

CHAPTER 1

the nearest we have been to any land since we left the English Channel (See 24th day July 5th) except the Cape de Verde islands. Many of us were disappointed in not seeing the Tasmanian coast.

Our position at noon was 44° 53' S, 145° 9' E. Run 190 miles.

Tuesday September 16th (97th day).

A light breeze and frequently heavy showers.

Shortly after 12 noon, we were greatly excited by seeing a sail on our port bow and as sailors and emigrants lined the bulwarks it seemed as though none of us had seen a ship before, and did not expect to see another. We have not seen a sail since August 3rd. The ship we sighted today was supposed by the sailors to be a small coasting schooner.

Position 44° 13' S, 148° 31' E. Run 160 miles.

The wife of an emigrant named McKenzie was today confined of a daughter.

Wednesday September 17th (98th day).

Wind light and sea calm. Having now rounded Tasmania we are steering three points farther to the north. We are now distant about 1200 miles from Wellington. The sailors took down the mizzen royal yard[32] on Saturday and the fore royal yard today, which signify the end of our long journey. As I write this Polly is knitting, Fred is fast asleep and Charlie is

---

[32] The 'royals' are the topmost sails.

singing the "Better Land." I hope his song may be a good omen.

Mr. Warner and I stood a long time on the deck tonight, watching the strange phosphorescent lights that appear to glow a little below surface of the sea; there are thousands round about us, varying in size apparently from the size of a saucer to eighteen inches in diameter. The sailors say the phosphorescence is emitted from a jelly-fish and is frequently seen in these latitudes.

Position 42° 47' S, 151° 8' E. Run 150 miles.

All the patients left the hospital today. The doctor says that so many are affected it is now impossible to carry out any method of segregation. It really looks as though he considers the *Douglas* to be a plague-smitten ship. My opinion however little it may be worth, is quite the reverse. I think the *Douglas* carries a lot of emigrants to New Zealand that will compare favourably with and previous arrivals, and possibly with any who may come after us. I don't believe there has been a case of either smallpox or fever on board. Six infants under a year old have died not from any infections but solely for lack of comfort and nourishment.

Thursday September 18th (99th day).

Light breeze and pleasant weather. The sailors have been scrubbing the paint work of the various structures on the main deck, and tidying up the ship in other ways so as to present a respectable appearance when we get to Wellington.

Position 41° 30' S, 154° 30' E. Run 170 miles.

Chapter 1

Friday September 19th (100th day).

Moderate breeze during the night; and improved gradually towards morning, all day it has blown strongly and we seem to have travelled at a fair speed. Nothing to record except that the general clean up goes on as yesterday.

Position 40° 57' S, 157° 11' E. Run 130 miles.

Saturday September 20th (101st day).

Various winds ranging from calm to gale. We have been busily engaged cleaning up our berths and surroundings in order to pass with credit, the inspection we expect to be subjected to on arrival at our destination.

Five albatross were caught by the doctor this evening, they are the most beautiful birds I have seen, four are brown and one grey. The smallest measuring ten feet across the wings and the longest twelve feet.

Position 39° 39' S, 161° 39' E. Run 208 miles.

Sunday September 21st (102nd day).

I think we have finer weather, today than at any during the last six weeks. General muster on the poop this morning when each emigrant had to respond when his name was called from the roll. The captain then read that portion of his log dealing with the insubordination of the young men in the 6th *inst.* and told them that in all probability proceedings would be taken against them on arriving at Wellington. Divine service at 11 a.m.

Our position is now 40° 20' S, 164° 3' E. Run 120 miles.

We are now running on the verge of the "roaring forties"; we have been in these latitudes, during a large portion of our eastward course.

Monday September 22nd (103rd day).

Pleasant breeze. The sailors are still busy cleaning the painting of the ship outside and woodwork on deck. The anchors that have lain on the forecastle since we cleared the English Channel, have been slung over the ship's side today. I am told this must be done as soon as we are within 300 miles of land: We are that distance from Rock's Point in the province of Nelson, New Zealand.

Position 40° 50' S, 166° 37' E. Run 125 miles.

We are now on the same meridian as the west coast of Otago.

Tuesday September 23rd (104th day).

Another dull showery day, but the breeze has been good and we have made good progress. I notice that a great change has taken place during the last few days, in our relation to each other, we are in better spirits than we have been for many a week and almost as pleasant towards each other as if living on shore. The ladies have been busy making, mending or improving sundry articles of dress and as I write 7.30 p.m. they are still at it, stitch, stitch, stitch; even the less decorative are ferreting out their holiday best as if determined to appear to advantage when they arrive at Wellington.

Chapter 1

The mate told us at noon that we were only 60 miles from land and at 4.45 p.m. Cape Farewell was sighted; as we drew nearer the coast the scenery was superb, a range of mountains seemed to come down almost to the water's edge and, far as the eye could see, peak after peak rose, while others higher and more distant lifted their snow-capped summits almost to the clouds. The sun was now setting and as the snow covered mountain tops reflected the tints of the clouds above the beauty of the scene can be better imagined than described, but as darkness set in, the scene was lost to view. The light on Cape Farewell was plainly seen from dusk till late in the evening.

Position 40° 6' S, 171° 18' E. Run 208 miles.

Wednesday September 24th (105th day).

The weather being very dull this morning we saw no land till afternoon when D'Urville's Island was sighted, and afterwards Steven's Island. These islands, more especially the former, appear rough and mountainous and are sparsely inhabited. We have passed through Golden Bay and Tasman Bay and are entering now the narrowest part of Cook Straits. Golden Bay was originally named Massacre Bay by Tasman, as some of his sailors had been killed there by the natives, but as the first New Zealand Gold was found near its shores, its name was changed to Golden Bay. The position and run of the ship not given. Tasman Bay was formerly known as Blind Bay having been so named by Captain Cook, but the former name is generally used.

Thursday September 25th (106th day).

Land, Land, Land. I am quite unable to do justice to the scenes witnessed today. Shortly after midnight I came on deck and saw the light on the Island of Mana: and again about 4 a.m. when almost dark I could distinguish the island itself which seemed to be unpleasantly, if not dangerously near, its dark, beetling cliffs seeming to rise like an immense wall within a few feet of the ship. At 5 a.m. the scenery was magnificent on our right lay the province of Nelson and on our left the province of Wellington, on the Nelson side the spurs of the Tairawhiti range formed the coast line and, as far as the eye could reach, as on Tuesday so today, one mountain peak above and beyond another, till the highest were lost in the clouds, the time the sun was just rising and as recorded on the 23rd *inst.*, "their snowcapped summits reflected the tints of the clouds above." On the Wellington coast the mountains were of less magnitude.

As we sailed on, the land on our right gradually disappeared. We were now going along at a fair speed, and at about 11 a.m. we arrived off Wellington Heads, a pilot was signaled for and shortly afterwards, when coming on board was greeted with rounds of hearty cheering. By this time the wind being against us – we were obliged to "heave to" and signal for a tug and waiting for a couple of hours, the *Lady Bird* came out to bring representatives of the Board of Health, and perhaps with the intention of towing to the anchorage or to the wharf should the health prove satisfactory, but this hope was soon dispelled. The chief medical officer of the Board put several questions to our

Chapter 1

ship's doctor, who in reply gave him to understand that smallpox and fever had been prevalent during the voyage, what arrangements were made with our Captain and doctor I have not learned, but while the conversation was proceeding and before we were made fast to the *Lady Bird*, a favourable breeze sprung up rendering her assistance unnecessary, and the good ship *Douglas* plowed her way in to the bay 'in gallant' style, where we dropped anchor at 4.30 p.m., after a passage of 106 days, or reckoning from the day we came on board, 107 days.

I shall never ever forget how anxious we were to see the New Zealand capital. There were 400 of us, not including the crew of about 50 who had not seen land for four months, gazing through the drizzling rain for the first sight of the empire city, it was raining, but nobody cared for that. Tea was ready and we were hungry for we had not had a meal since early morning, but nobody wanted tea. The all absorbing desire was to see Wellington: and when the cry was raised "Wellington in sight", I think the majority of us had each a fit of temporary insanity.

The evening was spent by most of us in walking the deck, and studying our surroundings with deep interest. We are anchored close to Somes Island near the centre of the bay, where according to report, we will have to go into quarantine for some time.

Friday September 26th (107th day).

We have all been busy this morning cleaning up our quarters in view of our official visit from the Health Officers and others, and at 11 a.m., we saw the boat making for the ship, and also another boat with provisions; we were disappointed however when they altered their course and headed for the island, where the Health Officers and inspectors held a large conversation with the captain and the doctor of the *Douglas*, the result being that we are to go into quarantine, and occupy the barracks on Somes Island. We are surrounded by sea birds of various kinds that greedily devour any scraps thrown overboard. We had no dinner today, as we refused to draw our allowance of pork, and the fresh provisions have not yet been issued.

Saturday September 27th (108th day).

Thank God, we have once more set our feet on *terra firma*. During the forenoon we were ordered to tie up our bedding in order that we might proceed on shore, the order produced great excitement and confusion, as everybody raced for a place in the first boat. The disembarkation began about noon, but it was not till about 3 p.m. that our boat got away. On landing we had first to carry our bedding and other impediments, along the beach to get fumigated, and then along a bad road, made slippery with the late rain, and running up a steep hill 300 feet high, on which the barracks stand, and before this was accomplished it was six o'clock in the evening.

Having had no dinner we made an excellent tea; and being very tired we spread our bedding on the floor and my wife, myself, and our two boys, retired for the night.

CHAPTER 1

Sunday September 28th.

Today is labelled "Sunday" on the calendar, but it has not applied to Somes, island. As the cooking for eleven families has all to be done at one fire, I extemporized a cooking arrangement for our own use; the effort was fairly successful, and enabled us to get a decent dinner, without the bickering that went on elsewhere. As the coppers will be required by the married people as soon as possible: the single men were ordered to wash all their underclothing and blankets today.

Mr. Powell (see June 15th 1873) gave a useful and interesting address this evening.

Monday September 29th.

Our present quarters are a great improvement on those we occupied on the *Douglas*. We no longer suffer from the rolling and pitching of the vessel; we have greater privacy, plenty of elbow-room, and plenty of good food. From the window of our room we can see the town of Wellington. The barracks are not yet quite completed; they stand on a small island in the harbour about 300 feet high and are built entirely of wood. We are the second lot of emigrants who have occupied these buildings.

Tuesday September 30th.

Somes Island is distant about five miles from Wellington and near the centre of the harbour; in extent it is between 70 and 80 acres, and on this land until quite recently a flock of sheep were grazing, but at present the livestock consists of about a dozen sheep, a few goats, and 400 emigrants. On the north side of the island there is a small grave-yard where about half a dozen people are interred. There is only one tombstone, on which is inscribed: "Sacred to the Memory of Mary Elizabeth Pudman who died 25th July 1872."

On the opposite side of the island is the lighthouse and nearby is the keeper's house and offices: this is the only house on the island.

Ferns and curious looking plants of various kinds, are plentiful. The harbour abounds with fish and some nice shells are found on the beach: among them were mussel shells in profusion, some of which were eleven inches long.

Wednesday October 1st.

My wife and I took the children to the beach this afternoon where we enjoyed ourselves gathering shells and admiring the scenery around us.

Thursday October 2nd.

Today the emigrants' boxes have been brought ashore, and everything we had on deck during the voyage has to be fumigated tomorrow. Most of the day was spent in sorting out our belongings as they came ashore and stowing them away in a shed.

Friday October 3rd.

My 33rd birthday. All the boxes that were supposed to need fumigating, with others that had never been out of the

CHAPTER 1

hold, were brought out of the shed and put through the fumigating chamber; those left on board the *Douglas* will be taken to Wellington and put on board the steamer on which we are to travel to Napier. I suppose a similar arrangement has been made on behalf of those who are booked for other ports. Those who are to proceed to Napier, number about eighty persons.

Saturday October 4th.

My wife has been washing today, my part of the business being to carry water and attend to the fire: there was so much bickering about the precedence that we neither used the copper or tubs provided the purpose. Our washing was done, the water being boiled in our mess-tins and fire-place was extemporized by means of a few bricks hastily thrown together and the entire operation was carried out most satisfactorily.

Sunday October 5th.

We had no public service today. In the afternoon we took the children to that part of the beach near the lighthouse and in the evening we went as far as the graveyard. We discovered the *Douglas* lying snugly at the Wellington wharf, where she had been berthed during the night.

Monday October 6th.

At sea, Paddle steamer *Luna*. We were called this morning at an early hour, and those who were booked for Napier were told to make all possible haste, as we had to muster on the jetty for inspection at 8 a.m. and at 9 a.m. the steamer would arrive to take us to our destination. This unexpected news appeared to be too good to be true nevertheless we began at once to bundle up our bedding, clothing and various odds and ends, and get them down to the beach without delay. This was no easy matter for it had rained during the night and the path was so slippery that it was with difficulty we kept our feet. At last the task was accomplished, but instead of 9 a.m. we had to wait till 2 p.m. before the steamer arrived. The inspection was a farce.

Figure 16 The government paddle steamer *Luna*. Thomas and his family travelled on the *Luna* from Wellington to Napier in 1873. (Photographer: David Alexander De Maus 1847–1925, National Library of New Zealand, item 1/2-014954-G).

We were all soon on board and almost immediately, started the last stage of our long journey. The evening being fine most of us walked the deck as we steamed out to the

Chapter 1

Heads, but no sooner had we passed out into the open sea than quite a different experience befell us. We had to face the head wind and a choppy sea; the little steamer was tossed about like a cork, and the smell of the machine oil was not conducive to inward peace.

We lay down in our clothes, but could get no sleep: a number of young people are singing under the fore hatch, and while we admired their fortitude, we are not in a position to follow their example, for the seas are breaking on deck, and every time this happened, the water finds its way into our compartment; there is nothing for us but to exercise patience and hope for the best.

We are journeying to Napier on the Government paddle steamer; *Luna*; under Captain Fairchild. The number of emigrants transhipped from the *Douglas* and now aboard the *Luna*, is 87.

I brought out my credentials as a Methodist local preacher and this I posted from Somes Island to the Rev. Wm Morley, Superintendent of the Wellington Circuit. I had a pleasant surprise when I was told that Mr. Morley was on board the *Luna*, bound like ourselves to Napier.

Later in the evening, I met Mr. Morley[33], who told me he was going to Napier at the wish of Conference; there is no Wesleyan church there although there are a few Methodists, and Mr. Morley is to find out, and report to next conference,

---

[33] This chance meeting with Rev. Morley was fortunate indeed. In due course, Thomas would be instrumental in setting up the Methodist church in Napier.

whether, in his opinion, it would be prudent to station a minister there.

Tuesday October 7th.

We have passed a stormy and sleepless night, and today there has been little change in the weather. The land appears to be less mountainous than that previously seen; neither did we see many houses as we steamed along the coast. About 3 p.m. we passed Cape Kidnappers,—two rocks, or small islets near the entrance of the bay, and distant about 15 miles from Napier. Here we got out first view of the town, which stood out with increasing clearness as we steamed across the bay.

We arrived at our destination about 4 p.m. and our boxes and baggage were got on the wharf as quickly as possible, and after the waiting drays had been loaded up, our belongings were forwarded to the Emigration Barracks. Up to a comparatively recent period these barracks had been occupied by the military, but recently they had been cleaned and put in order to receive emigrants coming to Napier under Sir Julius Vogel's Emigration Act.

Mr. Hebden met us at the port, and had very kindly procured a cab for my wife and the boys. I returned to the *Luna* for my overcoat, but on reaching the wharf I found that the boat had put off and was leaving for Wellington; there are papers in the pocket of my overcoat of great interest to me, and I will wire the boat at Wellington, though I fear I will not see them again.

Chapter 1

Mr. Hebden accompanied me to the barracks, is not now in business, but he can procure me work elsewhere. I am a little disappointed but will hope for the best.[34]

---

[34] Thomas did later find work with New Zealand Railways.

2. Travelling from New Zealand to England in 1901

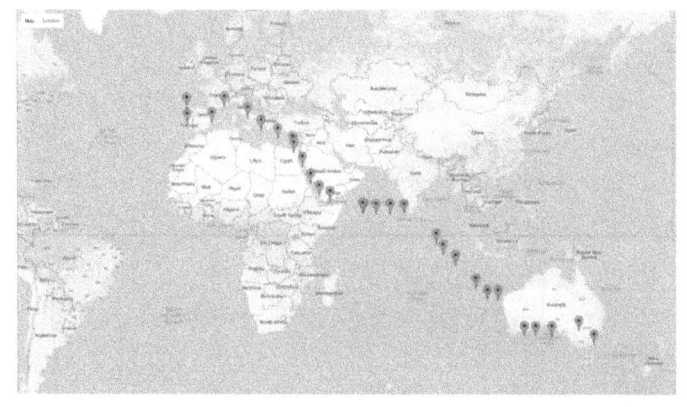

Figure 17 Daily positions of the RMS *Ormuz* on the voyage from Australia to England in 1901. (Courtesy Darrin Ward and Google).

Friday May 31st, 1901.

Left Napier this morning[35] by the express and arrived at Wellington at 8 p.m. The journey was uneventful as I have

---

[35] Twenty eight years have elapsed since the end of the previous chapter.

travelled over the ground on numerous occasions, but I was interested in that part of the machine that runs up the Rimutaka, where the gradient is so steep that it requires two powerfully constructed engines, specifically built for this purpose, to take the train from Cross-Creek to the summit, a distance of eight miles. This part of the line is built with a centre grip-line on the principal of some of the Swiss Railways. The incline runs between lofty spurs of the Rimutaka Range and, being in many places cut out of the cliff, we often had a deep precipice or towering cliff on our left hand as we travelled along. [36]

We got to Wellington as stated about 8 p.m. where we were met by my son Fred and various members of the Trevor Family, and were taken to Courtenay Place where Mrs. Trevor resides and where we were hospitably entertained. Later in the day a wire arrived from my sister Sallie, now in England, conveying the sad news that her husband, Mr. George Dodds had passed away at his home in Newcastle on April 1st.

Saturday June 1st.

Spent the night at Mrs. Trevor's and during the morning my wife and I had a look around the city, where we called on Mr. Ralph Draper etc., and in the afternoon Mr. Trevor and I drove to the wharf, where I got my ticket for Sydney, and from the wharf to the Athletic Park, where we witnessed a football match in which my son Fred played centre three-

---

[36] The railway ceased operating in 1955. The route is now a cycle path.

quarters. After tea Mr. Trevor and I had a look around, and at 10 p.m. I went on board the Union Company's boat *Warrimoo* and at 12 midnight we left for Sydney.[37]

Figure 18 Two special locomotives pull a passenger train up the steep Rimutaka incline. (Photographer: Roland Searle 1904–1984, Museum of New Zealand, from Wikipedia).

---

[37] His wife remained in New Zealand.

Chapter 2

Sunday June 2nd (3rd day).

I am very sea sick, never left my berth. We are now in the Tasman Sea and every wave that strikes the ship makes her shiver from stem to stern.

Monday June 3rd (4th day).

Conditions precisely as yesterday.

Tuesday June 4th (5th day).

The heavy sea encountered on Sunday and yesterday has gone down considerably, and I have felt considerably better. During the afternoon I was able to get on deck, but towards the evening the sea again was high and I was just as bad as ever. In fact the night was the most miserable as any I have had on board.

Wednesday June 5th (6th day).

Heavy sea and had another miserable day. About 7 p.m. we sighted Sydney Heads, and an hour later we entered the harbour said to be the finest in the world. We steamed on at a swinging rate until, just as the clocks were striking nine, we dropped anchor at the Union Company's wharf and were tied up.

The *Warrimoo* is a very swift boat but fearfully unsteady. The food is good and well cooked and plenty of it, and if a passenger is well he has little to complain about, but no consideration is given to anyone suffering from sea-sickness, the idea evidently being that if a passenger is not well, he ought to be. A sea sick passenger may lie in bed the whole day while crossing the Tasman and get neither sympathy or attention unless he has some friend to look after him.

Figure 19 The SS *Warrimoo*. Thomas sailed on her from Wellington to Sydney. (Photographer: Allan C. Green, National Library of Australia item 49210917, from Wikipedia).

Thursday June 6th (7th day).

Slept on board the *Warrimoo* and after breakfast in company with messieurs Kelly and Harvey – two fellow passengers who are also bound for London – we had lunch at Ellis Coffee Palace in King Street. We then saw our luggage safely across to the Orient Company and afterwards came up to the Office and got our tickets. I then took the tram to Enmore and found Mr. J. Coulson, a former local preacher in Napier, who now has a large furnishing store in

Chapter 2

Enmore Road. Mr. Coulson and I then called on Mr. Stairmond – another former Napier Methodist, who moved to Sydney a few years ago, and is now commencing business there. He left New Zealand on account of his health, which does not seem to have improved since leaving Napier.

After having tea at Coulson's, I went again to the Orient Company's Office where I was told that owing to some case of small-pox having occurred on the journey the whole of the crew had been quarantined and no passengers would be allowed on board until the vessel had been fumigated and passed by the Medical Board of Health. In the meantime we are to be provided with Board and Lodging at the Company's expense and I, with some others who came over in the *Warrimoo,* are to stay at a boarding house in Jameson Street.

Friday June 7th (8th day).

Spent the night at Jameson Street, where both food and accommodation are very indifferent. After breakfast I went to the Railway station where I took the train to Petersham in order to call on Mr. Richie, late a local preacher in the Napier Circuit, and we had further conversation on life in Napier.

After Mr. Richie had left us Mr. Coulson and I visited the sugar works where I was introduced to a number of his friends who, like myself, had formerly belonged to Darlington. Mr. Coulson and his friends were particularly kind, but I regret to say that I was not greatly interested in the things I either heard or saw. Got back to Jameson Street about 6 p.m., and spent the evening in writing to my wife and daughter Florence, 'Floss'.

Saturday June 8th (9th day).

Got all my luggage on board the *Ormuz* and after bidding Mr. Coulson and friends good bye, we steamed away on our long voyage.

Figure 20 The RMS *Ormuz*. Thomas sailed on her from Sydney to London. She was claimed to be the fastest ship in the world. (Photographer: Alan C. Green, State Library of Victoria, item H91.325/453).

About noon the weather was beautiful and Sydney harbour was seen to advantage as we steamed out into the open sea. We saw many villa residences as we steamed out, some well up on the banks, others in the sheltered valleys,

Chapter 2

and others again near the water's edge, but all adding to the charm of nature. As we passed the quarantine station our fellow passengers, left from the *Ormuz* and booked for their respective ports, stood waiting to give us a hearty cheer as we passed, to which we as heartily responded, and about 6 p.m. we passed out into the open sea. The evening being lovely and calm, I walked the deck until 10 o'clock and then turned in for the night.

Sunday June 9th (10th day).

Rose about 6 a.m. and walked the deck until eight when we were called to breakfast. I was expecting there would be a dining service during the voyage, but such was not the case. The day has been delightfully fine and the sea as smooth as glass. I have had no further indication of sea sickness and fervently hope that the worst is over.

Our position at noon was 38° 02' S, 149° 04' E. Distance run from Sydney 292 miles. We had then covered more than half the distance to Melbourne, where we expect to arrive about noon tomorrow. Wrote to my dear wife tonight and hope to post tomorrow.

Monday June 10th (11th day).

We arrived off Melbourne heads during the night and lay off till daylight. The weather was cold and drizzling as we steamed towards the wharf during the night, a distance of 60 miles. It was after ten a.m. before we got moored, and as soon as this was done I took the train to Flinders Street, where I had no difficulty in finding Mr. Edgar Newlands –

my wife's nephew, whose place of business is in "The Block" and known as the 'Atlas Press'. The business is on a very extensive scale, and Mr. Newlands is in no doubt doing well.

I was a little disappointed with Melbourne, but I saw it under adverse conditions the day being wet and disagreeable, and after spending an hour with Mr. Newlands I returned to the *Ormuz* at 3 p.m.

Flinders Street Station is fairly large, but in its architecture it is severely plain except at the main entrance where there are two or three ornamental structures. The carriages are dirty and poor; in other ways they resemble those in England, with the doors opening into the compartments from the railway platform.

Figure 21 Flinders Street Station in 1895. (Photographer: William Henry Jackson, Library of Congress, item wtc.4a02679).

Chapter 2

Tuesday June 11th (12th day).

Took in a large amount of general cargo and also several passengers and cast off from the wharf at 2.30 p.m., thus beginning the third stage of our sea journey. A good deal of amusement was given by a theatrical company who came down to the wharf to say goodbye to certain members of the company who were leaving for other parts, some appropriate songs were sung, and the drollery that was displayed by other members of the party was greatly enjoyed by all who were present.

The day has been very cold, with occasional showers of rain and sleet.

Wednesday June 12th (13th day).

A heavy sea, weather very cold and showery; the boat is rolling a good deal, and though I am not able to get out of bed I am not at all sea sick. Wrote to my dear wife, also to Mr. E. Banks a fellow workman.

Position 33° 44' S, 143° 3' E. Run from Melbourne 288 miles.

Thursday June 13th (14th day).

The weather moderated a good deal during the day, and at daylight we anchored at Adelaide and are lying probably about three miles from the shore, and steamers are running to and fro, but not having any business to do on the shore, I decided to stay on board and save my 4/6 for the return trip.

NEW ZEALAND TO ENGLAND IN 1901

Figure 22 The promenade deck of the *Ormuz*. (Maclure and Co. London, Robert Laws Collection).

I was much interested in the coaling of the vessel. Two laden coal hulks came off from Adelaide, one of which laid on each side of the *Ormuz*, thus enabling the vessel to take on coal on both sides at the same time. The men employed on this job work like Trojans, but the way they handled and ate their food was enough to make a dog sick. After coaling for a couple of hours, they were called to breakfast which consisted of bread and German sausage washed down by a liberal supply of coffee. With the meat and bread they made sandwiches quite two inches thick, and with unwashed hands as grimy as the coal they were handling these grimy sons of toil sat tearing and eating their food like as many gorillas. After the sandwiches, they had bread and butter washed down by pannikins of coffee. Then the inevitable smoke and off to work.

CHAPTER 2

Several ships are lying near us, and hundreds of gulls are flying round. I tried to see what Adelaide was like by using the binoculars, but I was not successful. A large number of passengers who came on board today are bound for Fremantle[38] where we expect to lose about one third.

We left Adelaide about 2 p.m., the weather was particularly fine and the boat steady. Posted letters at Adelaide for Mrs. Laws and Mr. E. Banks, shortly after leaving I received a letter from wife's brother Mr. W. H. Newlands, Bookseller and Stationer Castlemaine. Mr. Newlands visited us in Napier some years again and is the father of Mr. Edgar Newlands of Melbourne. See also June 10th.

Friday June 14th (15th day).

At sea in the Great Australian Bight. Another fearfully rough day and consequently a great deal of sea-sickness on board including myself.

Our position is 35° 32' S, 132° 31' E run from Adelaide 303 miles.

Saturday June 15th (16th day).

Another rough day and a deal of sea sickness on board. I managed to get up to every meal, but with this exception I kept in bed; this was partly owing to the day being wet and the boat rolling so much that I was afraid to risk walking on

---

[38] Thomas consistently writes 'Freemantle', but this has been edited.

the slippery deck, but apart from this I considered it better to keep in bed. We are now passing through the Great Australian Bight.

Our position at noon is 35° 32' S, 126° 10' E. Our run for the last 24 hours 310 miles.

Figure 23 The *Ormuz* in rough weather. (Artist: I. R. Wells, Illustrated London News, Robert Laws Collection).

Sunday June 16th (17th day).

Lay in bed all day, could not look at food.

Position at noon 35° 29' S, 121° 48' E. Run during the last 24 hours, 310 miles.

Monday June 17th (18th day).

We had a tremendous rough sea during the night and up till noon, when it moderated a little and I was able to be on deck for a while, but about 4 p.m. the sea rose again and I was compelled to go below and was just able to write a brief note to my dear wife, which I hope to post at Fremantle tomorrow. I then turned in for the night.

CHAPTER 2

Tuesday June 18th (19th day).

On awakening this morning, I found we were anchored off Fremantle, and after breakfast, I took passage in a small launch and went ashore. Fremantle seems to be a busy place, having a large breakwater and plenty of wharf accommodation, at which many large ships and steamers are lying.

Figure 24 Fremantle in the early 1900s. (Photographer: unknown, City of Fremantle Local History Photographic Collection, item 1278, from Wikipedia).

From Fremantle I took the train to Perth and was pleased to see that the engine had been made by Robert Stephenson and Co. Engineers, Newcastle on Tyne, and numbered 2887. The train accommodation is very good, the first class being nicely upholstered, the arm rests being to turn against the side when not otherwise required where they lay flush with the back. The second class were also cushioned and upholstered with brown tapestry. The Australian Railways, so far as I have seen, are all on the broad-gauge principle. Those I saw today were divided into five compartments with two seats in each, and each seat capable of accommodating five passengers, or fifty to each carriage. The doors are at each end as in England.

There are some decent little places between Fremantle and Perth, but the land is poor. Perth itself is one of the prettiest towns I have seen in Australia, and business seems to be brisk, but everything seems to be very expensive. I paid 1½d each for apples and 3d each for oranges. The buildings, as might be expected, are much inferior to those at Sydney, Melbourne, or even to those at Auckland, New Zealand.

Mr. Ford, a New Zealander, gave me a letter of introduction to a friend of his named Sedgwick, but on calling I found he was away from home. I therefore gave the letter to Mrs. Sedgwick. I then took the special train to the *Ormuz*, and arrived on board a little after noon. Soon after this she finished coaling and at 2 p.m. we started for Colombo, and shortly after, we passed Rottnest Island on which there is a penal settlement, and soon after we were in the open sea. As I write (5.30 p.m.) the wind is blowing cold, and the sea a little choppy.

I had a long talk tonight with a passenger named Bell, who knows Mr. Trevor well (Fred Laws married his daughter) in fact it appears they were neighbours living in Cleveland in 1873. His name is Thomas Bell and is going to Newcastle to visit his two sons, who are in business as builders at Heaton, a town on the Tyne a few miles below Newcastle. I am the bearer of a letter from Mr. Trevor to an

CHAPTER 2

old friend of his named Smalley, who lives at Thornaby near Stockton-on-Tees. Mr. Bell says he knows this gentleman well and is well acquainted with the entire family, so I gave him Mr. Trevor's address and he has promised to write.

I see by a Fremantle paper that the *Astral* was unable to communicate with the shore at Adelaide yesterday; this was no doubt from the effect of the same storm as we encountered on Sunday and Monday last. It is also stated that three of the *Astral*'s passengers died on the voyage owing to excessive heat.

Wednesday June 19th (20th day).

We had a calm sea during the night and the *Ormuz* made good progress. I arose about 5.30, and after a good bath I went on deck till breakfast time. After breakfast we met the P and O boat *Oceana* and were so close as to easily distinguish her name. I learn today that so rough was the sea when passing through the Bight that for 24 hours the captain never left the bridge except to take a little refreshment. The sea smashed the door of the doctor's cabin and nearly washed the doctor out of bed, and one of the sailors was nearly washed off the saloon deck. Tonight I spent hour at the doctor's Bible class, though there were only three of us present: the doctor, a Wesleyan passenger named Emerson and myself.

We are now entering the Indian Ocean, position at noon 23° 43' S, 111° 40' E. Run since leaving Fremantle 313 miles.

New Zealand to England in 1901

Thursday June 20th (21st day).

The sea has been a little lumpy, and though not yet quite recovered from the effect of my sea-sickness, I am beginning to get my sea legs and my sea stomach. Our position at noon was 23° 43' S, 107° 25' E. Run 354 miles. We are now entering the tropics. Saw a few flying fish.

Friday June 21st (22nd day).

The weather is now getting warmer and I am hoping to have got over my sea sickness, for although the boat has rolled a good deal today, I have felt very little inconvenience, and no sign of sickness.

The passengers on the whole are a rough lot, but there are a few decent fellows among them and the following are the names of the few I have chummed up with: Joseph Gilbertson going to Walton near Liverpool, Robert Gorst from Queensland going to Ulverston, W. S. Harvey from New Zealand going to Thurso, Scotland, John Smith from New South Wales going to Tow Law, County Durham, L. Solier, a Frenchman from Victoria to St. Malo France, Peter Kelly from Dannevirke, New Zealand to Limerick Ireland, James Brown from Dannevirke, New Zealand to Plymouth, England, Thomas Bell from Otago, New Zealand to Newcastle on Tyne.

Position at noon 19° 36' S, 102° 54' E. Run 353 miles.

Wrote to George Earney tonight

CHAPTER 2

Saturday June 22nd (23rd day).

The heat is now becoming tremendous, though sometimes tempered by a cooling breeze, the old boat is still going steady and we are making good progress.

Our position today is 15° 26' S, 98° 43 E. Run since yesterday at noon 345 miles.

Sunday June 23rd (24th day).

Arose about 4.45 a.m. and enjoyed the luxury of a saltwater bath. At 11 a.m. Divine service was held on the upper deck, the captain reading the Church of England service for the day; one of the stewards presided at the organ and the ship's band was in attendance, the weather was beautiful, and the *Ormuz* was as steady "as a painted ship upon a painted ocean."

The weather is getting hotter and all on board are now dressing as lightly as possible, many of the male passengers going in their bare feet and wearing neither coat or waistcoat. I have stripped to the singlet, and in addition am wearing only pants, drawers and shoes.

Our position at noon was 11° 19' S, 94° 52' E. Run not given.

Monday June 24th (25th day).

The sky was overcast this forenoon and the day has been fresh and breezy. We had our first allowance of lime juice today. Wrote to my brother Bob.

Position at noon 7° 25' S, 9° 11' E. Run 320 miles.

Tuesday June 25th (26th day).

We are now well within the tropics, and the heat increases as we proceed north. We now get lime-juice twice each day. I have written up some of my lantern slides today, this being the first opportunity I have had since leaving New Zealand. Several tropical showers have fallen today.

Our position at noon was 3° 17' S, 87° 28' E. Run 333 miles.

Wednesday June 26th (27th day).

Crossed the Equator at 2 a.m. and at noon were 350 miles from Colombo, where we expect to arrive tomorrow. The weather is fine.

Our position at noon was 1° 05' N. Run for the last 24 hours 340 miles.

Thursday June 27th (28th day).

We had a nasty rough sea today, and lots of the passengers who had been all right since leaving Fremantle, have again suffered from the effects of *Mal de Mer*. I was not particularly sick but suffered from a nasty head ache, and am greatly out of sorts and terribly seedy.

Shortly after noon we came in sight of "Ceylon's Isle", and sailing along the coast, arrived at Colombo about 8 p.m.: the land we passed was generally low, though fairly sized hills were frequently seen. As soon as we had tied up, many of the passengers including myself and two or three chums went ashore and were lucky to find a native guide who had been in

Chapter 2

Australia and spoke English fluently, and with him for our guide we strolled through the town and also the native quarter. I think the town like Jerusalem of old, is "Beautiful for situation" and the most interesting that it has been my privilege to see.

The streets are wide and in good order and are of a dull brick-red in colour. The lighthouse is a conspicuous object and stands on a gentle rise in one of the main business thoroughfares, and on the opposite side of the street in one of the longest and most fashionable hotels. The town is lighted by electricity and has a good electric car service.

We have arranged with Joseph, our guide for a three hours' drive tomorrow, when we hope to visit various places of interest. We sleep tonight at the British India Hotel, Galle Face Road and are to pay each 2/6 for bed, 2/6 for breakfast and 2/6 for the dinner including horse and conveyance. It is said that baksheesh (tips) are to be provided for, but so far we have neither seen or heard of this imposition.

Friday June 28th (29th day).

The night was very hot therefore we did not sleep well, we were certainly not burdened with bed clothes one sheet only being allowed to each bed. Our room was large airy and communicated with a verandah by means of wide folding doors, the opening between the posts being filled in with diamond trellis, as I attempted to show on the previous page (Figure 25) but failed owing to lack of the necessary tools, but through which we could look upon the sea which was quite near.

for breakfast, and 2/6 for the driver including horse and conveyance. It is said that backsheesh (tips) are to be provided for, but so far we have neither seen or heard of this imposition.

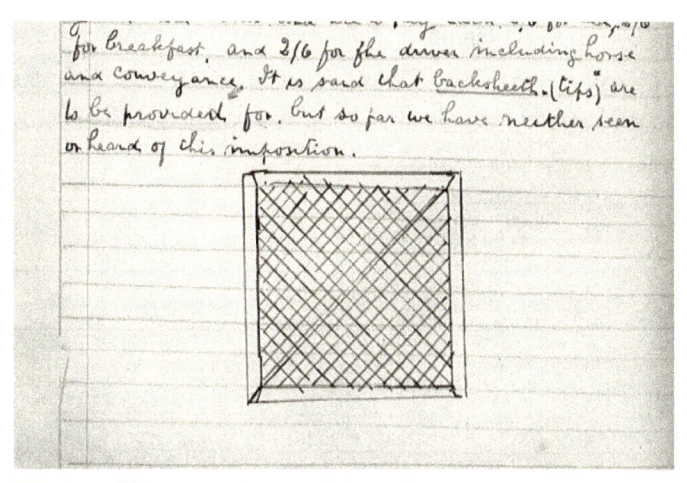

Figure 25 Thomas's sketch of the trellis. (Laws Family Collection).

I was awakened at daylight by the cawing of the rooks with which the place seems to swarm, their colour being black except on the back, which is a light slate colour, and the size of the bird, about that of the English Jackdaw. At 6.30 we had breakfast which consisted of fresh sausages, eggs and bacon, potato chips, bread and butter, tea and coffee. There was also an abundance of fruit: oranges, mangoes, bananas and others that I am not able to name.

We were waited on by natives, but as the native men and women dress so much alike we were for some time in doubt as to which sex our attendants belonged. There was no sign of either whiskers or beard, they had long black hair, which was held back by a semi-circular comb. They were good looking, gentle in speech and manners, slender in build, about five feet high, and wore long, loose, white garments. No wonder we were in doubt whether we were being attended to by a couple of young ladies, or fellows of the

CHAPTER 2

baser sort[39]. At length our doubts were set to rest by Mr. Emerson asking one of them fair and square to which sex they belonged. We were then assured that our attendants were only men like ourselves.

Figure 26 Colombo street scene in about 1900. (Photographer: unknown, location of original: unknown, from Wikipedia).

Saturday June 29th (30th day).

About 7 a.m. our guide of yesterday came with his horse and carriage, and we were soon off on our excursion. After taking us through some of the principal streets, we got to the suburbs where the wealthy Europeans live: many of the villas were exceedingly beautiful, not so much on account of their architecture as of their setting, for besides being spacious

---

[39] 'fellows of the baser sort' is an expression taken from the King James edition of the bible, Acts 17:5.

they stood in large well-kept orchards in which grew an abundance of large tropical trees both fruit and ornamental and most beautiful flowers, and climbing plants in all their beauty and variety covered the walls as high as the second story windows. The roofs are covered with red tiles the bottom row being laid with its hollow side upwards.

We then went to part of the town named Slave Market, but why this name I was unable to discover.[40] There is here a large fresh water lake, around which the natives swarmed, a great number were simply walking about as though out for a holiday, many were carrying umbrellas as though to protect them from the fierce heat of the sun, others were carrying burdens of various kinds generally upon their heads, some were driving bullock carts, some running along with the rickshaw – a light two-wheeled carriage drawn by one man. There were old people and young people, some in full dress and others almost nakèd, children of all ages and conditions and on all sides the incessant cry was "give, give", as we rode along these mendicants followed us like bees they took upon themselves to explain things of no moment and then asked for payment.

Children thrust their little hands into ours and asked for money, a cripple hopped alongside our conveyance showing his withered limbs and asked for money. If you looked into a shop window, a man off the street would come along, after talking a little while he would volunteer to point out something he considered to be of interest and expect to be

---

[40] Under Portuguese rule, there was a market selling slaves taken from Portuguese East Africa.

CHAPTER 2

paid for the service he had rendered. Umbrellas, walking sticks, carved elephants, spectacles, waist-belts and other thing would be pressed upon you by half a dozen vendors at the same time. One man – his face wreathed in smiles asked me if I knew of anyone who would give him something, and I was compelled to acknowledge that I was not acquainted with anyone who had a weakness in that direction.

Figure 27 A bullock cart in Colombo in about 1900. (Plâté and Co., Robert Laws Collection).

Most of the children are really pretty, and their voices so soft and plaintive that it is hard to refuse them any request they make. I was fairly adopted by a little girl about ten years. We were looking round the native market, when she took me by the hand, saying "Pappa, Pappa, I'se glad I'se found you Pappa, please give me something" and looked into my face so beseechingly that for once I was obliged to yield to her blandishments, release her affectionate grasp, and steal back to the carriage.

Coco-nuts were growing in all directions: the trees in full bearing would be about 25 feet high and a crown of fern-like leaves shooting out around the top and underneath the leaves. The nuts grew in profusion of perhaps 50 to each tree. The foliage in the garden was the freshest green, and the flowers being abundant, large and beautiful in colour made a picture that will not soon fade. The bread fruit trees were much smaller and had a bright green leaf, not unlike the ordinary laurel. I saw no perfect fruit on these trees, all I saw were quite green and shaped about the size and shape of the ordinary hazelnut. Bananas were growing everywhere and the fruit could be obtained in every degree of perfection, but they were much smaller than those we get in New Zealand. I saw no mangos growing, but the fruit is plentiful and cheap in Colombo. There were many other kinds of fruit with some of which I was familiar, while there are others of which I had not even heard the name. One of the latter resembles a horse chestnut which, on being cut in two, was found to contain a delicious, white, pulpy substance.

The lake referred to is 14 miles long and winds in and out among the trees and some of the little bays are very beautiful. Several men were fishing, and a large number of both sexes were washing their clothes, by simply dipping them in the water and washing them on the large stones that lay upon the shore.

We next visited the Cinnamon gardens, and literally enjoyed the spicy breezes that blow from Ceylon's Isle, the wood has a pungently aromatic odour. I have no idea how many cinnamon trees there are in the garden, but they are very numerous and fairly large.

CHAPTER 2

Figure 28 Washing clothes at the lake. (Photographer: William Henry Jackson, Library of Congress, item LC-D4271-269).

We were next shown what we were told was the largest Banyan Tree in Ceylon, the drip of the tree was said to be 100 feet, but the universal opinion in our company was that it was much larger. At distances of ten or twelve feet, smaller vines or rootlets let themselves down from the branches and on reaching the ground, in the course of time, take root and become fairly large trees that support the parent branch from which they have come. This process is repeated all over the tree as long as it continues to grow. Some of the supporting branches had become trees from six to eight inches in diameter and varying in size according to their respective distances from the parent stem, those being the first to descend, being of course much larger than what came down several years later. This curious growth was strangely interwoven and formed a maze of beauty difficult to describe. From what has been said it will be understood that, from near the parent stem to the outside of the tree, these downward-growing branches grew gradually smaller. The larger ones were like pillars that supported the heavy horizontal branches, while those forming the outside circle were not much stouter than ordinary pieces of whipcord.

The foliage in the gardens was the freshest and brightest green I had ever witnessed, the flowers being large numerous and gorgeous. It made an impression that will not soon be effaced. There are some beautiful walks and drives that bear historian names: such as Hyde Park Corner, Regents Park, Victoria Park and others.

From the Cinnamon Gardens we next visited the Temple of Buddha, which stands on the shore of a lake. Here were scores of natives, presumably Buddhists, loitering about the building, there was no service going on, nor was any reverence manifested either for the building or for the Buddha. The one object that seemed to be possessed by young and old was expressed in the universal cry "give, give." We were soon surrounded by clamorous crowd who followed us from room to room all the time we were in the temple their one object evidently being to get all the cash from us that could possibly be extracted. I verily believe the great image of Buddha itself could have been purchased.

The temple is void of all architectural beauty. It is a low, heavy lumbering whitewashed building, clumsily plain, outside and within. The interior of the temple seems to consist of several small, ill proportioned rooms averaging about 20 feet x 10 feet though the room in which the pulpit

Chapter 2

stood would probably be about 20 feet square and open on three sides, the roof being supported by wooden pillars. The sacred tree of Buddha is called the Bo-tree, there is nothing peculiar about the appearance, but there is a legend that it was under one of these trees that Buddha rested for the night, but under what circumstances I was not able to get any information. The tree is quite common, and there are dozens of them in the Cinnamon Gardens.

In the first room we entered were several images of Buddha, great and small, all arranged along one end, and a young man carefully explained the nature of each, but his English was so imperfect that his eloquence was thrown away.

He kept repeating the words "My lord Buddha" over and over again and before we came out we were asked to put something in the cup for charity, which we did, and we each in addition purchased a Buddhist prayer, written on a palm leaf. We then came into the courtyard, where in a separate building a larger image of my lord Buddha was kept, and where we again listened to another unintelligible lecture from our quondam friend, which none of us could understand. In front of this idol, were laid the offering of flowers, brought hither by his devotees. We were shown the pulpit and were told the priest preached from it every new moon, and then our young friend asked for his fee, but as we had already given for charity and bought a prayer the request was declined. After leaving the temple we drove away followed by our young friend for more than a quarter of a mile until, probably realizing that our charity was unequal to meet this further demand, he returned to the temple a sadder and wiser man.

We visited the native market, where we bought some fruit that was neither good nor cheap, and the haggling and chatter that went on between the vendors and his customers was very amusing.

The native carts are drawn by diminutive oxen, and it is astonishing to see the heavy loads they draw. It seems as though horses are few in Colombo. The ordinary road traffic does not suffer on that account, but the odour of oxen is so prevalent that I marvel it has been allowed to go on for so many generations, but though the streets are kept scrupulously clear the offensive odour continues especially in the native quarter.

We were advised "never to give a native more than half the price he asked for any article" and this rule worked fairly well though many articles changed hands for considerably less. While we lay here the natives literally took possession of the ship, they swarmed like bees everywhere, all sorts of things were brought on board and offered for sale:- fruit, umbrellas, walking sticks, boxes made of cinnamon wood, cats' eyes and other precious stones, gold rings, hammocks, carved ivory elephants, and many other things, and each tried to sell his wares, but I am pleased to say that I saw no pilfering by either the crew or passengers though the opportunity was sufficiently numerous, and wares were handed round so promiscuously, that some of them could have been easily hidden away, this was sometimes done in pretence, but never with dishonest intention.

One man had lost a carved elephant and he was running

Chapter 2

about the deck, crying like a child, and saying "I lose my elephant, I lose my elephant", but it was given back, and he was soon all right again.

An Indian fakir came on board, and did some clever tricks. He would have given us an exhibition of snake charming, had he been more liberally patronized. Although delighted and interested with all I have seen at Colombo, I will not be sorry to get back to the ship which I did about noon, and we steamed away on our voyage at 3 p.m. while the diving boys on the wharf were singing "The Soldiers of the Queen." (Figure 29).

Saturday June 29th (30th day).

At sea in the Indian Ocean, weather fine though exceedingly hot. The captain is steering a more southerly course than usual in order to avoid the adverse monsoon that blows more adversely this month than at any other time of the year.

I am told this is the worst month of the year in which to cross the Indian Ocean.

Position at noon 7° 42' N, 75° 0' E. Run from Colombo 282 miles.

Sunday June 30th (31st day).

Divine service was held on board twice today prayers being read by the captain in the morning and by the doctor in the evening when he also preached from John V.12 "He that hath the son hath life." The morning service was a very

NEW ZEALAND TO ENGLAND IN 1901

formal affair, but I believe the doctor is a good Christian man. Anyhow we had a much better service in the evening.

Weather fine, position 7° 49' N, 69° 43' E. Run 325 miles.

Figure 29 'The Soldiers of the Queen', a song celebrating the prowess of the British soldier in the days of Empire. (Author: Leslie Stuart 1863–1928, National Library of Australia, item 172099105).

CHAPTER 2

Monday July 1st (32nd day).

There has been a heavy sea running, and a nasty hot wind blowing all day, but I did not feel very well so after breakfast. I went to bed and did not get up again till 4 p.m. By looking at the position of the boat during the last few days, it will be seen that we have been running nearly due west.

Our position today being 7° 56' N, 64° 21' E. Run 319 miles.

Tuesday July 2nd (33rd day).

The weather seems to be getting worse; we are now in the SW monsoon and the boat is pitching as badly as when we were crossing the Great Australian Bight. I am not sea-sick but positively unwell: my head is swimming and I can neither eat or sleep. We have not seen a ship since we left Colombo, and the same dull round goes on day after day. The usual games lack interest, very few can settle themselves to read, and the passengers stroll about the deck or lie about the hatchways. Cards, dominoes, and drafts are bought out, but the games are short-lived. Sometimes you will see a passenger gazing listlessly over the bulwarks for a long time until, tired of the sameness, he mechanically walks over to the other side and takes up a similar position where the same scene presents itself. "Water, water, everywhere", he has changed his position, that is all. A flying fish or a seabird may be seen occasionally, but even that is now unusual.

When coming out in 1873, we saw whales, sharks, Portuguese men of war (a kind of nautilus I believe), Cape pidgeons, Cape hens, albatrosses and other birds, but during the present voyage we have not seen any of these.

Position 8° 11' N, 59° 33' E. Run 286 miles.

Wednesday July 3rd (34th day).

The boat has rolled terribly today and I have had a bad time and kept in bed most of the day. I saw the doctor this morning who gave me some medicine which he says will do me good.

Our position this morning was 8° 11' N, 59° 8' E. Run during the last 24 hours 263 miles.

Thursday July 4th (35th day).

The sea continued rough until about 11 a.m. when it moderated considerably, although the weather is lazy, several of the passengers declared they could see land on our left, which proved to be Cape Guardafui and was now plainly seen by all. The land is not very high, I would say at a guess not more than 70 feet or 80 feet above sea level with a belt of sand between it and the sea and getting more extensive as we sailed on. We were are only about half a mile from the land and with the aid of our binoculars, we had a fairly good view of that portion now within range of our vision. There are a few scrubby bushes, and large boulders scattered over the surface, but not a sign of human life appeared. We are now in the straits of Bab-el-Mandeb and the sea is unmoved by a ripple, and every-body seems to be in better health and spirits.

CHAPTER 2

Position at noon 11° 12' N, 51° 44 E. Run during the last 24 hours 258 miles.

Friday July 5th (36th day).

The quiet sea noted yesterday continued till this morning, but today it has been rough again, until by 11 a.m. it was as bad as ever and continued to get more angry the farther we got into the Arabian Gulf.

Our position at noon was 12° 30' N, 46° 30' E. Run 329 miles.

Saturday July 6th (37th day).

We passed Aden at midnight and at 2 p.m. entered the Red Sea. The weather is very hot, though tempered by a nice breeze, and the sea is a smooth as glass. During the forenoon we passed several small islets the names of which I could not obtain, but at one p.m. were abreast of the group known as the Twelve Apostles, a number of small barren rocky Islets said to be twelve in number. Today we have seen a number of steamers some going eastwards and others towards the west. Tonight there was a concert on deck, but I remained below and wrote up some of my lantern slides.

Position at noon 14° 43' N, 42° 18' E. Run 334 miles.

Sunday July 7th 38th day).

After a good night's sleep I got up at 4 a.m. and had a delightful salt water bath and then went on deck till breakfast. The morning was beautiful and a nice refreshing breeze was blowing and the boat as steady as a house. At 10 a.m. we met the *Orizaba*, one of Orient liners, and gave her a cheer, to which her crew and passenger as heartily responded.

There was Church of England service, both morning and evening, but I did not attend either as I was too busy writing letters to my dear wife, Mr. C. G. Cunnold, Mr. George Warden, and others.

Position at noon 19° 3' N, 39° 2' E. Run 352 miles.

Monday July 8th (39th day).

I am surprised that we see so little land. I expected that when passing up the Red Sea we would have seen land on one side or the other almost every day, but it was not so: we saw a little yesterday and just a mere speck today. Very early this morning an Arab dhow was seen in the distance and about 10 a.m. we passed another. I had a good look at both through the glass and was astonished to see such a great, lumbering sail being carried on so small a vessel.

During the last few days, there has been a good deal of dissatisfaction among the third class passengers about the quality of the food and the way it is cooked and served, and this culminated today in their sending a petition to the captain signed by 47 of those interested.

Position 24° 48' N, 35° 53' E. Run 356 miles.

Tuesday July 9th (40th day).

I arose at 3 a.m. and had a look at the island of Shadwan as we passed, and at daylight we were well within the Gulf of

Chapter 2

Suez, with land on both sides of us and a belt of sand running down to the sea, beyond this was a low mountain range. The sunrise on the Arabian coast was almost worth coming from England to see. The mountain peaks were tinged with deep purple and the clouds assumed such a variety of shapes and colours, the beautiful blending being simply indescribable.

Figure 30 An Arab dhow in the Suez Canal in about 1900. (Goodyear Archival Collection, Brooklyn Museum).

At 7 p.m. we passed the unsightly lighthouse on Cape Ashraf and as we proceeded further up the gulf the land on both sides increased in barrenness. Instead of sand lying in level patches as we would naturally expect it, the surface was rough and rugged and thickly studded with sand hills of every shape, size and colour. There were several telescopes in

New Zealand to England in 1901

operation, but no sign of life either human or otherwise was visible.

We arrived at Suez at 2 p.m., and anchored two or three miles from the town. I counted 14 sails coming out to meet us and all had their canvas spread; they made picture. Each sail had a crew of three or four Arabs and it was not long before the deck of the *Ormuz* was crowded with these swarthy boatmen, as at Colombo it was with Singalese. Our visitors today were equally glad to dispose of their merchandise, but to their honour be it said that I saw no one begging for money

I regret to say that I can neither compliment passengers or crew on their conduct towards those poor Arabs. When writing on the day we spent at Colombo (June 28th), I said "no unfair advantage was taken of the natives either by crew or passengers.", but today the Arab boatmen were considered fair game for plunder and ill treatment. They were robbed and hustled by the cowardly firemen, pelted with any dirt that came to hand, and subjected to such indiscretions as made me for once regret that these offenders and I were fellow-countrymen.

The Arabs were far less demonstrable than the Singalese. The wares they were selling consisted of dried figs, grapes, dates, shells, coral, parrot fish, sun fish, eggs, feathers, and other sundries of a like nature.

At 3.30 the bell rang, and our visitors were soon into their boats and off to Suez. Suez is built on the edge of the desert and appears to be a typical Eastern town; the old town is still a native quarter. The houses are low, flat roofed and flanked by heavy-looking square towers. There are several

Chapter 2

mosques, easily distinguished by their domes and minarets. Although there is so much sand – sand everywhere and so little black soil – I was surprised to see so large a number of trees growing in the streets. The new town on the European quarter is nearer the anchorage and contains the mercantile establishments and offices of the canal company.

We entered the canal at 4 p.m., and had a good look at Suez as we passed. The buildings are all modern and in the European style and generally painted some light colours, such as light blue, French grey or white. Groups of Arabs were squatting under the trees or conversing by the side of the canal.

A statue of Lieutenant Waghorn is placed at the eastern entrance to the canal. I am told he was the first European to superintend the transit of mails across the isthmus. The banks are low, and as the desert stretches on each side of this great waterway as far as the eye can reach the scene is a barren and uninteresting as it is possible to conceive. On the right, as we entered, was a small native settlement with several camels lying about, the natives with their long flowing robes and head gear of turban and fez made a truly oriental scene that reminded me of the Bible pictures I was familiar with when a boy.

About 15 miles from Suez we came to the Bitter Lakes. In the canal proper, we are not allowed to travel at a greater speed than five miles per hour, but when in the Bitter Lakes, where the water may be anything up to 20 miles wide, the vessels can proceed at their maximum speed.

The channel is marked here by buoys painted red and white, and by means of these the boat is kept on her course.

A lamp that burns compressed gas is attached to each buoy and which burns night and day keeping the course open at all hours. The quantity of gas in the cylinders burns for six weeks night and day without being recharged, this arrangement being cheaper than extinguishing and relighting.

The *Ormuz*, having an electric projector, was allowed to proceed during the night when the buoys are distinguished as clearly as at midnight. We tied up for a short time at Ismailia to change pilots, and the night being fine I remained on deck till midnight.

Position at noon 29° 36' N, 32° 33' E. Run 341 miles.

Wednesday July 10th (41st day).

When I came on deck at 5.30 a.m. I found we were still in the canal and about 14 miles from Port Said. Lake Menzalah lay on our left about a mile distance, the intervening space being covered with vegetation on our right was still the hot, monotonous desert. At 7.30 a.m. we arrived at Port Said, which was a pleasant relief to the eye after so much sea and sand. On our right was still the desert.

Port Said, though much smaller, is as like Colombo as one English town is like another. The buildings with few exceptions are low and flat-roofed. The offices of the Company are housed in a larger building and stand out prominently among those of smaller size. It has three domes and, being painted a light French grey, looks cool and pleasant to the eye. Hundreds of Arabs (or Egyptians) were walking about or squatting on the wharves, and a number of small boats were lying with awnings spread, and quite a

CHAPTER 2

number of large ships were lying at the various wharves; some coaling, and others taking in or discharging cargo.

Figure 31 The *Ormuz* navigating the Suez Canal at night using her electric projector. (Illustrated London News, Robert Laws Collection).

The system of coaling is different from any I have seen elsewhere. Two planks were run out from each side of the *Ormuz*. By one comes the coal from the hulk to the bunker and by the other the empty buckets are returned for a fresh supply, the men walking so close to each other that they remind me of an endless chain of which every man is a separate link. There are a number of men whose duty it is to fill the baskets and place them at the bottom of the gangway and these men never leave the hulks while coaling is going on. The carriers pick up the loads, convey them to the bunkers, empty them, and return to the hulk by way of the other plank. The men go at a jog trot all the time and all move as regularly as a piece of clockwork. Port Said has the reputation of being the quickest coaling station in the world. On this occasion we took in 500 tons in three hours.

Figure 32 Coaling a steamer at Port Said in about 1900. (Library of Congress, item LC-M32- 810).

It is now reported that bubonic plague has appeared on the *Ormuz* and that one or two of the passengers are affected, and we were not sure if we would be allowed to land, but notices are now put up prohibiting any passengers or members of the crew from landing. There is no coaling to be done nor are any on board to leave the ship.

CHAPTER 2

So we were under way again at 11:30 and in a few minutes were out in the Mediterranean. Before clearing the Canal, we passed a large bronze statue erected to the memory of M. de Lesseps and after about an hour's steaming we could see the masts of the vessels as they lay in the harbour at Alexandria and the lighthouse lying a little further to the west.

Position at noon 31° 30' N, 32° 3' E. Run from Port Said 18 miles.

Thursday July 11th (42nd day).

There is nothing of particular interest to write today. At 2 p.m. we could discern the Island of Crete away to the north, and from that till 8 p.m. we were sailing along the coast, but owing to the distance and the haze we could see little. At 2 p.m. we passed a small island on which there is a lighthouse, but we were not sufficiently near to see more than this cliff on which it stood. Wrote letters to Mabel, H. Mole, and my wife all in NZ, also to my brother Jack and Mr. Willis in England.

Position 34° 01' N, 26° 16' N. Run 334 miles.

Friday July 12th (43rd day).

The sea at noon was the smoothest I have yet seen, there was not the slightest ripple. The water has been a beautiful deep blue, the like of which, I am told, is not found except in the Mediterranean. We saw several steamers as we held on our way but no land.

Position 36° 34' N, 19° 38' E. Run 357 miles. The best run since we left Sydney.

Saturday July 13th (44th day).

We passed through the Straits of Messina during the night and therefore saw nothing of the scenery. I have read and heard so much about. At daylight we had the Sicilian coast on our left and passed several small islands. We are now off Stromboli and have a good view of the mountain, which we pass at the distance of about a mile and a half and was seen to advantage as it is not particularly high—at a guess I would say about 2000 feet—and in shape somewhat resembles Mount Egmont, in New Zealand.

A large town, the name of which I could not find out, is on the north west of the island and is almost immediately under the volcano. With the knowledge of what befell Pompeii, I was surprised to see the town in this position. The mountain was clothed in verdure right down to the water's edge. At 8 p.m. we came in view of the Italian coast and have been running along the Calabrian coast nearly all day. This part of Italy is the most picturesque and also the most fertile land I have seen on this journey. I have not forgot what I wrote about Colombo and the Cinnamon Gardens, but there is a difference between the beauty of a landscape and the beauty of a city, and in this case I think the honours are about equal.

At 11 a.m. we first caught sight of Vesuvius between two cones of a nearer range, a column of smoke was rising from the crater and hovering cloud-like over the mountain top. At

Chapter 2

11.30 we were between the island of Capri and the mainland. It was at Capri that Garibaldi lived and died after the accomplishment of Italian Unity.

As we drew near to Naples, villa residences became more numerous: the hills were terraced to the top and in places the houses almost came down to the sea-shore. We had now a perfect view of Vesuvius; it is a beautiful sight with its sloping sides coming down to the seashore and Naples sleeping at its feet. It was not till we entered the bay that we began to see the fine architecture for which the city is famous.

The town extends around the bay and grand villa residences and other fine buildings line the shore as far as the town extends. As distance diminished the town was seen to better advantage following the generally accepted dictum that "distance gives enchantment to the views." The upper part of the cove was covered with congealed lava and therefore destitute of vegetation, but the lower slopes were fresh and green and houses were dotted here and there right up to the lava. The Railway built by Cook and sons runs up the mountain side almost to the summit, the station being on the spur about half way up.

The castle of St. Elmo occupies a commanding position. It was here the Royal Family resided before the Unification of Italy. It appears to be a very large building though outwardly very plain. The houses are away from the business part of the town, and being on the rising ground command a splendid view of the bay. Most of them stand in orchards or vineyards and all are noble buildings.

As soon as we anchored, a dozen small boats came alongside, but none were allowed to come on board as information had reached the authorities that we had bubonic plague on the vessel. Up to this time we had heard nothing of this except rumour to that effect at Port Said, but the yellow jack was now run up and this settled the matter.

Water police were now sent to patrol the boat, and neither crew or passengers were allowed on shore and the coaling had to be done from the lower ports, which prevents any of the coalers from coming on deck. Fruit sellers and vendors generally are not allowed to come near the vessel, but in spite of these restrictions they sometimes manage to effect a sale. On one of the boats are some minstrels who sang and played the mandolin and other instruments, and on another are some sisters of mercy, who beg the passengers to throw gifts in the their inverted umbrellas, but to this appeal I fear there was poor response.

There was one patient taken ashore this afternoon and was said to be suffering from smallpox, but of this I only heard a rumour. It is currently reported that we are to be quarantined here for ten days, these flying reports are sometimes realized, but just as often prove to be without foundation.

Naples has a population of nearly half a million.

Position 40° 21' N, 14° 27' E. Run 370 miles since yesterday.

CHAPTER 2

Sunday July 14th (45th day).

We are still lying at Naples, and I have little to add to what I said yesterday: at 10:30 and Vesuvius is throwing out volumes of smoke right in front of us.

Figure 33 Vesuvius, at about the time that Thomas saw it. (Photographer: William Henry Goodyear 1846–1923, Goodyear Archival Collection, Brooklyn Museum Archives item S03_06_01_024 image 3120, from Wikipedia).

The coal barges came alongside at 6 a.m. and coaling went on till 7 p.m. This is by far the slowest business of the kind I have seen and is in marked contrast to our friends at the other end of the canal. Where (as I have already told you) we took in 500 tons in three hours. The most of those employed here are mere lads, and instead of each carrying and emptying his own basket the men stand in a row and the baskets are passed from hand to hand, neither do they use shovels as at Port Said, but a kind of triangular hoe is used, by which the coal is dragged into the basket. There is said to be about 200 men and boys employed in this work, but they lack the system displayed by the men at Port Said.

Although the water police patrolled the boat all day the dealers managed to do good business by watching their opportunity, so that when the police were at one side of the boat they made a dash for the other and in this way got rid of their merchandise. The articles offered for sale were toys, fancy baskets, fancy boxes, musical instruments, fruit, and alabaster goods in great variety.

From a conversation I had with the doctor, it is not likely that quarantine will be imposed upon the ship unless there are many fresh cases of infectious disease, and that he fully expects to reach London on July 22nd according to timetable.

The boat finished coaling at 7 p.m. and left for Marseilles at 9 p.m. I am not able to say what quantity of coal was taken here, but at Port Said as already stated 500 tons were put on board, and probably the same quantity was put on board at Naples. If these figures are approximately correct, the case stands as follows: Naples for 13 hours' work 500 tons of coal taken in. Port Said for 3 hours' work 500 tons of coal taken in.

As we steamed away, our electric lighting showed brilliantly around the shores of the bay, and up the slopes beyond, but the scene was as brief as it was interesting for, going at full speed, the lights were soon lost to view and beautiful Naples left far behind. Naples with its historic associations, its beautiful setting of the green hills behind, and the Bay at its feet, and the scene crowned by the grand, though dangerous, Vesuvius is a sight never to be forgotten.

CHAPTER 2

I can see a striking resemblance between Napier and Naples, though it (Napier) lacks the historic associations and the volcano. The bay, though smaller, is of similar configuration and equally beautiful in shape and proportion. The hills on which the better class of houses stand are as a rule equally green, and rather than recommend my friends to "See Naples and die" I would rather "See Napier and live."

Monday July 15th (46th day).

Nothing of interest occurred today. From midday till 6 p.m. we were passing through the straits of Bonifacio, between Sardinia and Corsica. As seen from the boat, both islands appear to be mountainous and thinly populated. We saw a few isolated houses and one or two hamlets and a small town on the north west corner of the island. There were patches of cultivation, the dividing fences being clearly seen.

Corsica on the north side of the strait is similar in character, perched on the cliffs or nestling in the valleys a solitary house or a small hamlet may be seen as we pass on. Corsica is chiefly celebrated as being the birthplace of Napoleon the First.

Owing to a case of small-pox previously refereed to, nearly all the crew and passengers have been vaccinated either yesterday or today, a few are refusing and, for those who won't submit, a ten days' quarantine will be imposed when we arrive in England.

Position at noon 41° 15' N, 10° 4' E. Run since leaving Naples 200 miles.

Tuesday July 16th (47th day).

Went on deck at 5:20 this morning and found we were close to the French coast. Owing to the case of smallpox previously referred to, I now learn we are compelled to fly the yellow flag. At 6 a.m. the yellow was flown and the pilot came on board, and not being allowed to be at the wharf, we were taken to an anchorage a little distance away. I now learn that the mail for England was not put ashore at Marseilles and that the French pilot will have to proceed to London and will not be allowed to enter France until the government is satisfied that all danger of infection is past. We are greatly disappointed in not being allowed to land at Marseilles. We left Marseilles at noon and headed to Gibraltar where we are due to arrive on Thursday.

Position at noon 43° 16' N, 5° 14' E. Run from Marseilles 7 miles.

Wednesday July 17th (48th day).

At 10 a.m. we had our first view of the Spanish coast, and have not lost sight of it all day. So far it is rugged with little sign of vegetation, but that the country is fertile as reported I have no doubt.

About 6 p.m. we came perilously near running down a small schooner. It was quite daylight at the time and we passed with only a few inches to spare, there was a good deal of shouting and excitement on both vessels, but no damage was done.

Our position noon 38° 53' N, 0° 26' E. Run 343 miles.

Chapter 2

Thursday July 18th (49th day).

During the morning and afternoon we were sailing almost due west, and we saw several little hamlets as we swept along, the land is less mountainous and appears to be more fertile than that recently described. At noon the famous Rock of Gibraltar was sighted, but owing to the haze its outline was not seen till we arrived at the anchorage. We left for Plymouth at noon and so we had no time for investigation, but excepting the Rock there is not a great to see or to explain. It is 1,400 feet high, and the fortifications have hitherto been considered to be impregnable.

Since 1704 it has been in possession of the British. In 1779–1782 it withstood a memorable siege against the combined forces of France and Spain. The population is now between 15,000 and 16,000. Just as day was breaking we passed Cape Spartel, with its white lighthouse and soon afterwards Lake Trafalgar, for ever celebrated for Nelson's crowning victory over the combined fleets of France and Spain, October 26th 1805.

Friday July 19th (50th day).

Weather cold and foggy and the siren going at short intervals all day, and the boat going at half speed. Yet notwithstanding these precautions we nearly ran down a small fishing boat, which we missed by the merest shave.

We passed the Bay and City of Cadiz in the night and at 6 a.m. were opposite Cape St. Vincent the scene of another great victory by the British fleet on January 14th 1797, when Sir John Jarvis defeated the combined fleets of France and

Spain. After having rounded the cape, our course lay further to the north, and during the remainder of the day we were steaming along the coast for Portugal.

Our position at noon was 38° 25' N, 9° 30' W. Run from Gibraltar 278 miles.

Saturday July 20th (51st day).

Weather cold and foggy, and the siren going at short intervals all day, and the boat running at half speed, and this probably makes us a day late in arriving at London. We saw no land on account of the fog. At noon we were off Cape Finisterre, and rounding this point our course lay more to the eastward.

We have now given up all hope of getting into Plymouth tomorrow. The weather is damp and dull and truly represents our mental barometer according to present reading.

Position 42° 59' N, 9° 41' W. Run 272 miles.

Sunday July 21st (52nd day).

Weather still cold and hazy consequently very little land has been seen. We had a distant view of the lighthouse at Ushant and Brest as we passed. Ushant is a small island off the coast of Bretagne. We are still running at half speed in order to reach Plymouth at daylight tomorrow.

CHAPTER 2

Monday July 22nd (53rd day).

England, Dear old England.

> Breathes there a man with soul so dead,
> Who never to himself hath said.
> This is my own, my native land.

Came on deck at 5.30 a.m., and found that we had entered Plymouth sound and were slowly making for the anchorage. I cannot express my feeling in cold pen and ink, but when I first beheld the dear old homeland I instinctively took off my hat and mentally quoted the lines at the head of this paragraph.

The first thing that struck my attention, when I had time to look around, was the beautiful landscape on our left; this was a most welcome relief to the eye after going for so many weeks on ocean and desert. Instead of the unsightly wire fences as in New Zealand, I saw once again the hawthorn hedge: the hawthorn with its well-remembered white and fragrant blossom, and instead of the large paddocks, with only here and there a human dwelling, to see the fields in all their variety of size, shape, and colour, and the village churches, the villas of the wealthy and the cottages of workers peeping out among the trees or standing on the grassy slopes, as we proceeded to the anchorage.

The Health Officers and those of HM Customs were aboard almost as soon as we had anchored, and after the passengers had been inspected and their luggage passed, the steamer *Smeaton* took the passengers and their luggage ashore. There was a good deal of hand-shaking and cheering with a little weeping as we bid each other good bye, and handkerchiefs and hats were waved till the *Smeaton* landed her passengers at the wharf.

Two of the crew, said to be suffering from bubonic plague were, put ashore. These men had been in hospital since we left Naples, and if suffering as reported the plague must have been of a very light nature. They walked from the ship without assistance, and although one man appeared to be a little weak, the other skipped down the gangway and into the boat, as if nothing was amiss. While on board, everything was done to isolate these men from the rest of the passengers and crew, that part of the deck being roped off and one of the crew told off to keep watch. However, plague or no plague, we were examined by the Health Officers, and each had to leave their future address.

At 11.30 we left Plymouth and started on the last stage of our long voyage. As we steamed to the English Channel the scene was most impressive, hill and dale, fields gay with colour, trees decked in their summer foliage, and buildings great and small were passed in ever varying succession. All nature seemed to rejoice. We were all so delighted with the prospect of getting ashore tomorrow that a large number walked the deck all night and never went to bed.

Tuesday July 23rd (54th day).

We were all early astir this morning packing our boxes and preparing to go ashore. The weather was thick and hazy so that we saw little of English coast as we sailed along.

Chapter 2

About 10 a.m. we entered the Thames, and not long after having entered the river, we arrived at Tilbury.

3. Visiting Friends and Family in England in 1901

Tuesday June 23rd, 1901 (1st day in England).

All luggage was bought from the cabins, and each passenger was instructed to stand by his own. The custom house officer then came along and said which he wanted us to open and when this was done, if nothing of an incriminating nature was found, the luggage was initialled by the officer and could be taken ashore, which was done by a small steamer, and by 1.30 p.m. all passengers and their luggage had been landed where a special train was waiting. It took us a little while to sort out our belongings, but when this had been accomplished they were speedily transferred to the train, and, taking our seats, we were soon on our way to the Great Metropolis.

The brief railway journey had little interest as little was seen except warehouses, high chimneys and workmen's cottages, and I was glad when at 4 p.m. we got to King's Cross, where after having booked our luggage, Messrs.

CHAPTER 3

Smith, Gilbertson and I procured lodgings at Pearce's Hotel, Liverpool Street, and had tea. I then went to the house of an old friend named Edward Walker, where I spent the evening with him and his good wife. Mr. and Mrs. Walker and their two sons were ship-mates of ours when we came out to New Zealand in 1873, and after our arrival in the Colony we were assisted in many ways, especially in work, being both carpenters, and also in church matters, both being members of the Wesleyan Church. Mr. Walker, his wife and family returned to England sometime about 1895 or 1896 and we had a long talk about former times and mutual friends.

Wednesday July 24th (2nd day).

After breakfast went to the Bank of New Zealand where I got my draft cashed. I had some letters to deliver and a few calls to make, but as it rained heavily I decided to start for the North. I then went to the Great Northern Railways, where I presented a letter given me by Mr. Ronayne, General Manager of the New Zealand Railways, and Sir Joseph Ward, Minister of Railways, to the Company General Superintendent from whom I got a free pass "York Return" that left at 1:35 and got to York at 4 p.m. Here I parted company from Mr. John Smith who has been my fellow passenger on the *Ormuz* since we left for England. As the northern line terminates at York, I had to take an ordinary [ticket] for Darlington, where I arrived about 5 p.m. and then by cab to the residence of Mr. Willis, Mowden Terrace, to whom I delivered a letter and several small presents from his son, Mr. Luke Willis of Greenmeadows. I was hospitably entertained during the two or three days I remained at Darlington.

The news of my arrival quickly spread and soon several of Mr. Willis's friends made their appearance, and the remainder of the evening was spent in general conversation and distributing presents. Everything seen on the journey today reminded me of old times: the trees, the fields, the farm houses, and their surroundings. The factories, villages, cottages and towns, the rooks, robins, partridges, linnets, sparrows and other birds that I had not seen for 30 years, all spoke of old association and appealed to every fibre of my nature. The only unwelcome things I saw were huge advertising boards announcing "Derby Tobacco, Cadbury's Cocoa, Hudson's soap and Beecham's Pills." Why are these things allowed to mar the beauty of the landscape?

Thursday July 25th (3rd day).

This morning I again saw several of Mr. Willis's friends, and later Mr. Bishop and I had a stroll in the Public Park; this is a large and beautiful acquisition to the town: the grounds are most artistically laid out and the market gardening far exceeded anything of the kind I had previously seen. There were really some striking portraits of Her late majesty Queen Victoria, King Edward the VII, Queen Alexandra, the Duke and Duchess of York, and others. I had no idea that such work could be done with flowers just plucked from the garden. There is a nice sheet of ornamental water, an aviary, and a bowling green capable of accommodating several rinks.

Chapter 3

In the afternoon I took the train to Stockton-on-Tees where my wife and I lived for two years.

Figure 34 Heading north by train in about 1901. (Tony Hisgett Collection, licence CC BY 2.0).

I called on Mrs. Smally at Thornaby and on Mr. Wright at Norton Road, the latter being friends to Mr. James Trevor. I then visited called on Mrs. J. Huitson at Thornaby, where I had tea, and Mr. Huitson and I had a good look around the dear old town where I had spent three happy years. The new Commission Methodist Church and the Roman Catholic were familiar landmarks, also St. John's Anglican. The Railway station and the old Market Cross. I took a long, lingering look at the houses in which we had lived, the house no 18 Stamp Street was in no way changed, the doors being open I could see the stairs leading to upper rooms, and through the open passage the back premises were clearly seen except the fresh water aquarium which I had kept in the sitting room. We had lived in this house in 1871 and 1872.

VISITING ENGLAND IN 1901

I then had a look at the house no 2 Station Street, the house in which we were living before coming to New Zealand and this also we found in the same condition as when we left it in 1873, and as I stood and looked at these houses I moralized on the happy years we spent within them, on the hundreds of times we had crossed those thresholds, and the old friends I knew, but of whom with one exception I was not discover with the limited time at my command, the exception being that of Mr. Thomas Hind, my wife's uncle.

Many changes have taken place during the 28 years of my absence. As expected, many new warehouses and public buildings have gone up, the wide front street, however, remains unchanged, and the Vane Arms and the Red Lion still growl at each other from the opposite sides of the street. I got back to Darlington at 10.30 p.m.

Saturday July 27th (4th day).[41]

Spent some time this morning in visiting one of our Mission Rooms, Mr. Bishop having kindly offered to show me round and his daughter being the sister in charge. Here tramps and men out of work obtain cheap board and lodging and are surrounded by healthy moral influences calculated to lead them to a better life. Divine worship is held in a spacious room every Sunday and I am told it is meeting with a fair amount of success, attendance being strictly voluntary, and everything is scrupulously clean.

---

[41] Thomas's day numbering seems to go astray here.

CHAPTER 3

After dinner I went to the Railway Station, where I got a Free Pass, Newcastle – return. The journey was particularly interesting, and as we passed spots that were comparatively familiar my heart beat fast.

On arriving at the Central Station I hailed a cab, and after my luggage was put on board, we set off for my sister's at Bentinck Crescent[42]. I was familiar with every street and turn, and almost with every building as we drove along Westmoreland Street, Westmoreland Terrace, Westmoreland Road, up Rye Hill and along Elswick Road. We got to Bentinck Crescent about 5.30, and the first to welcome me to Newcastle was my sister, Mrs. ['Sallie'] Dodds, but there was an element of sorrow in our meeting that cast a pall over the long expected joy of our meeting. I had been looking forward to meeting her husband, whom I had never seen, but God had willed it otherwise. Her husband, Mr. Geo. Dodds RAM, had passed away on April 1st.

Notwithstanding her great bereavement, I found her wonderfully calm and resigned by the assurance that the meetings and welcomes awaiting us in the future when our earthly griefs and disappointments will be all forgotten.

Apart from this, we had a happy meeting. My sister said she knew me as soon as I stepped in, and I would have recognised her had I met her in the streets of London. As we sat and chatted, first my sister, Mrs. [Susannah] Coulthard,

---

[42] Bentinck Crescent is in Newcastle. In the 1891 census George Dodds and Sarah née Laws are listed as living at number 14 with children George and Herbert. This Sarah was always known as 'Sallie'.

and then my sister Mrs. [Elizabeth Jane] Thompson arrived, they had both altered in appearances considerably though I was able to recognize them without difficulty.

Figure 35 Thomas's brother John William 'Jack' Laws. (Robert Laws Collection).

My brother Jack was the next to make his appearance, he had gone as far as Darlington to meet me, but there were two trains leaving for Newcastle at the same time, one by

Chapter 3

Leamside and the other by the Team valley and in this way we missed each other. I would not have recognized Jack had I met him accidently, he is not only a deal stouter, but his features had altered considerably.

While we sat and chatted, my sister's two sons, George and Herbert [Dodds] joined us, and such an evening surely had never been spent either in England or elsewhere. We talked of, and some of us with, our children. We talked of our childhood, the games we played, of old scenes and associations, and of all that had happened since we parted nearly 30 years ago. It was late when we separated and I am looking forward to many such meetings before I return to what I must now regard as the land of my adoption – but Dear old England, with all thy faults I love the still.

Sunday 28th July (5th day).

The British Conference of the Wesleyan Methodist Church is at present meeting in Newcastle, and representative ministers are preaching in all the churches throughout the district. This morning I went to Elswick chapel with my sister, Mrs. Dodds, where we heard the Rev. Jeffries preached from John XIV, 8. "Show us the father and it sufficeth us." I cannot say that I was impressed by the sermon.

In the afternoon the Oratorio 'Athalie' was given by the choir in excellent style. My nephews George and Herbert Dodds being respectively conductor and organist. The attendance was large and appreciative. At 6 p.m. Dr. Watkins, one of the Australian delegates took the service, but the Doctor was far from being at his best and I think the sermon failed to grip.

Monday July 29th (6th day).

Before leaving New Zealand the Rev. C. E. Beecroft kindly gave me letters of introduction to several of his ministerial friends now attending the Conference, so I went to Brunswick Place Chapel hoping to see some of those to whom I had a letter from Mr. Beecroft, but I was not able to meet with any that I desired to see. I met Mrs. Gibson at Trafalgar Street and gave her the parcel sent by her son Mr. M. Spriggs of Napier. Took the train to Wallsend, where I expected to meet Mr. Willis of Darlington and his daughter, Mrs. McKay. But having gone to Tynemouth, they failed to materialize. I then returned to Newcastle and called on Mrs. Thompson, the local manager of the North British[43], to whom I handed the letter of introduction signed by Ronayne and Sir Joseph Ward.

I think he must have seen the word Wellington at the top of the sheet for he began to put me through a severe, examination as though I were applying for an old age pension or had come to borrow a five pound note, and he wound up by saying that it was not possible to grant it.

But when I told him that his was my first refusal he seemed to put on his considering cap and softened down a little. He then asked me where I had come from, and when I told him New Zealand, I saw his features relax. "Oh!" he

---

[43] The railway network that covered most of Scotland and extended into Northumberland and Cumberland.

CHAPTER 3

said "that is quite a different thing. I thought your letter was from Wellington in Shropshire, and you would go to Glasgow. All right I'll give you the pass." I then discovered that he had a very high opinion of New Zealand, and before parting he said that he was Presbyterian and the North British line went as far as Aberdeen, and he would be glad to grant me the necessary Free Pass.

I had tea in town and did not get to The Crescent[44] till after 6 p.m. There I found Amelia Bowes, George and Bert Dodds, Miss. Ella Wilson and my sister Mrs. Dodds, and we spent an enjoyable evening.

Tuesday July 30th (7th day).

Wrote several letters this morning and in the afternoon called on my aunt Elizabeth[45] who is living with her daughter in Dunstan Road. Before her marriage with my uncle, Mrs. Laws and I lived with my mother's aunt[46] in Ponteland for nearly 30 years so we had plenty of things to talk about in connection with our early days.

---

[44] Bentinck Crescent.

[45] Elizabeth Fletcher, one of the nieces adopted by Sarah Yeaman. Elizabeth later married Thomas's father's brother, John Dixon Laws.

[46] In fact she was Thomas's *father's* aunt, Mrs. Yeaman.

Figure 36 The Seven Stars Inn, where Thomas grew up. It stands between the former tea rooms and the former Albion Temperance Hotel. (Photographer: unknown, Ponteland Local History Society Archives, reproduced with permission).[47]

After tea I met my sister Mrs. Dodds near Grey's[48] Monument and we paid a visit to Mrs. Wm. Fletcher a half cousin of mine who had also been brought up by my great aunt Mrs. Yeaman at the Seven Stars[49] in Ponteland for

---

[47] These and more photographs of Ponteland can also be found in John Turner, Images of England: Ponteland, 1999, ISBN 0-7524-1806-8.

[48] Earl Grey, famous both for his tea and the Great Reform Act. The monument is 130 feet high and the public are allowed to climb its 164 steps, but it is generally fully booked a year in advance.

[49] The Seven Stars still stands.

CHAPTER 3

nearly 20 years, so we had plenty of things to talk about in connection with early days.

My mother's aunt, just referred to, is Mrs. W. Yeaman, who for many years kept The Seven Stars Inn at Ponteland. I was brought up by her and lived at the hotel from the time I was a year and nine months old[50], until she sold it in 1861. Her husband died in 1842[51], and having no children of her own she practically adopted three orphan nieces, named respectively[52], Mary, Elizabeth (Lizzy) and Sarah Fletcher, and a fourth niece whose father had died when she was very young, was also named Lizzy, who married my father's youngest brother John D. Laws, and is the Mrs. Laws that I visited this morning.

Of the three sisters just mentioned, Mary married Mr. W. Higham, and after living a number of years at Blyth died there. Elizabeth (Lizzy) married Mr. A. E. Common of Kenton Bank Foot, with whom I served my apprenticeship[53].

Mr. Common died some years ago and shortly afterwards his widow went to live with her married daughter at Heaton, near Newcastle where she still resides. Sarah Fletcher – the youngest of the three sisters – married her cousin William

---

[50] Thomas was therefore adopted sometime in July, 1842.

[51] William Yeaman died of a heart attack on 13 June, 1842.

[52] The census data from 1851 confirms most of this.

[53] An apprenticeship would have lasted seven years. It typically began when the child was about twelve to fourteen years old. Kenton Bank Foot is about three miles south east of Ponteland.

whose name was also Fletcher, her surname therefore was not altered.

After having spent an hour and a half with Mrs. Fletcher, my sister and I went to Clarence Street Wesleyan Home Missionary meeting. Mr. Gerald France, who is a son in law of Mr. J. B. Bowes, presided, and the principal speaker was a son of the late Rev. Luke Wiseman. The meeting was thinly attended and not very enthusiastic. I remembered I preached several times in Clarence Street Chapel while I was a local preacher living in Newcastle.

Wednesday July 31st (8th day).

Spent the morning at The Crescent, and in the afternoon I was present at the Foundation Stone Laying of the Westgate Hill New Mission Hall[54], when stones were laid by the following ladies and gentleman: Sir W. H. Stephenson[55], Mr. J. B. Bowes, Mr. J. C. Maudlin, Miss. Bambridge, Mr. Slack, Mr. A. R. Shaw, Mrs. John Jopling and Mrs. J. A. Potts. The building is estimated to have cost £20,000.

At 7.30, a meeting in connection with the Building fund was held in The People's Hall, Rye Hill, the chair being taken by Sir W. H. Stephenson, the speakers being The Rev. H. G. Pope D. D., T. W. Macdonald, and S. J. Collins. It was a good meeting. The chairman is one of the best known

---

[54] A grand Grade II listed building. It was a place of major relief to the local poor.

[55] Sir William Henry Stephenson (1836–1918) had been knighted in 1871. He was chairman of the Board of the Inland Revenue.

CHAPTER 3

Methodists in the North of England. He was thrice Mayor of Newcastle, is very wealthy and gives liberally to religious, charitable, and patriotic institutions. He is a local preacher, and class leader in connection with Elswick Road.

I was also pleased to meet my old friend and class leader, Mr. James Stobert[56] (Figure 37) of Ponteland, who was my Sunday School teacher from my earliest recollection, and when contemplating a visit to the Homeland I looked forward with joyful anticipation to the time when I should see his face, and take him by the hand. His features are not greatly changed, and although he looks a little older the intervening years have dealt kindly with him. We were mutually pleased to meet each other once more. We had a cup of tea together, after which I made my way to The Crescent, where I spent the remainder of the evening, and stayed all night.

---

[56] James Stobert 1825–1905. "James, a man of great stature, evidently had a charismatic personality. He inspired the development of Methodism in Ponteland in the latter half of the nineteenth century." From the booklet: Ponteland Methodism, published by Ponteland Methodist Church, 2001.

VISITING ENGLAND IN 1901

Figure 37 Thomas's friend and mentor James Stobert (1825–1905) photographed in 1898. He was fifteen years older than Thomas. (Photographer: unknown, Ponteland Local History Society Archives, reproduced with permission).

Chapter 3

Thursday August 1st (9th day).

Went to Brunswick Chapel this morning and was fortunate in seeing the Rev. Thomas Griffin and Walford Green, to whom I delivered Mr. Beecroft's letters of introduction, both were very busy at the time and we had little time for conversation, but I hope to see them again before conference closes. I had also a brief conversation with the Rev. Joseph Berry, who succeeded the Rev. J. S. Smalley as minister of Trinity Church, Napier, New Zealand, and is now one the Australian Representatives. I then crossed over to Gateshead were I spent some time with my dear brother Jack and talked over many things past, present and future, and after lunch we took the train to Sherriff Hill. I had often travelled this road when living at Eighton Banks 30 years ago and it has altered very little during the intervening years[57].

After our return to town, we had a stroll through Gateshead Park, which is very nicely laid out though greatly inferior to the one at Darlington. We had a long talk with the custodian, and I promised to send him some young cabbage-trees which he thinks he will be able to grow in the Park. We then had a look through the corporation offices, including the magistrates court and the council chambers, where my brother showed off the peculiarities of some of the councillors by mimicking their voice and gesture, until both sides of me shook with laughter. We then had a cup of tea

---

[57] In another copy of the diary he says "owing to trams, more houses, and other improvements, I hardly recognise it today."

together and I went to The Crescent, where I spent the remainder of the evening.

Friday August 2nd (10th day).

Mrs. Dodds and I went to Dunstan this afternoon, where we spent an hour with my sister Mrs. [Susannah] Coulthard and her husband. It was here that my sister Mary died in 1891, my father (Figure 38) in 1885 and my mother in 1891, their respected ages being Mary 45, Mother 77 and my Father 70. I got a good deal of information from Mr. Coulthard concerning the last days of those dear ones who have gone where there is neither sun or sorrow and "where God shall wipe all tears from their eyes." After tea we went to Elswick Road Chapel where the Fernley lecture was delivered by Rev. Tasker.

Saturday August 3rd, (11th day).

Met my brother in town this morning, and we had a look through the Hancock Museum, and we were delighted with all we saw, and I could not help contrasting all we saw with the miserable old museum that stood in Westgate Street 30 years ago. The Hancock Museum, contains the entire collections of birds and animals, as stuffed and set up by the late Mr. J. Hancock, and presented by his widow to the city.[58]

---

[58] Now called the Great North Museum. It still houses numerous antiquities and stuffed animals from the original collection.

Chapter 3

The collection is considered to be one of the best in the country. I was especially pleased to see several contributions from New Zealand, and Napier was represented by two cases, presented by G. H. Swan Esq., brother of Sir Joseph Wilson Swan, the inventor of the dry plate photography and the incandescent electric lamp.

Before leaving New Zealand I had been often told that, on account of alteration and improvements, I would hardly recognize either the towns or the villages I knew so well, but so far this has proved quite incorrect. The leading thoroughfares are today just as I remember them: Dean Street, Grey Street, Market Street, Clayton Street, Market Street, Grainger Street, Collingwood Street, Mosely Street, Northumberland Street, Percy Street, Gallowgate, and many others, are not altered in the least, and in not a few instances the same name, advertising the same business, is on the signboard.

The town has grown exceedingly since 1873, and many new streets occupy ground that was then in pasture or tillage. The same may be said of Gateshead, Stockton-on-Tees, Darlington and other towns I have visited, and probably of nearly all the towns in the country.

Figure 38 Robert Laws (1815–1885), Thomas's father. (Laws Family Collection).

Chapter 3

Sunday August 4th (12th day).

Heard the Rev. J. Burgess in Elswick Road Chapel this morning, and at the conclusion of the service the Rev. Sylvester Whitehead unveiled the memorial window in memory of the late George Dodds Esq who for 20 years had officiated as organist of this church. The window was presented by Sir William Stephenson and the subjects were chosen by his youngest daughter and also drawn by her. On the left panel David is represented with his harp, and on the left Miriam with her timbrel. It is a beautiful window, and shows in concrete form, the estimation in which the late organist was held by the church. Mr. Dodds was known far beyond the bounds of his town and neighbourhood. I have conversed with men of different views of religion and life, and all speak of his many excellences or write in testimony to his many virtues. Mr. Whitehead who had known Mr. Dodds for many years, and Sir William Stephenson, with whom Mr. Dodds had worked at Elswick Road for 20 years, joined in testifying to his capacity as an organist, and to his character as a Christian gentleman, and both speakers expressed the pleasure it gave them to know that he been succeeded as organist by his eldest son.

There lies before me as I write an old note book by which I find that on August 4th 1861, exactly 40 years ago today, I listened to four well known ministers in Newcastle: at 7.20 a.m., the Rev. David Hay in Brunswick at 10.30 a.m., the Rev. Morley Punshon in Brunswick at 3 p.m., the Rev. G. J. Perks in the Presbyterian Church, and at 6 p.m. the Rev. J. H. Riggs at Brunswick Place to an overflowing

Visiting England in 1901

congregation. It is a remarkable coincidence that after 40 years, 29 of which I spent in New Zealand, I should once more by spared to spend a Conference Sunday in Newcastle.

My brother Jack came in from Washington this morning, and was present at the service in the church, and also at the unveiling ceremony. We had dinner at The Crescent, and afterwards drove to Washington, where I preached from Luke XXII. 31. After service we spent a very pleasant evening, singing and chatting till bedtime. There were present: my brother and his wife, Mr. and Mrs. Dickinson, my nephews, Monty, Con and Norman and Mr. and Mrs. Dickinson's granddaughters – Gertie, Nellie and May Dickinson and my niece Helen.

Monday August 5th (13th day).

Came to Newcastle from Washington this morning. My brother and his wife only coming as far as Gateshead with the intention of meeting later at Rowlands Gill in time for the stone laying of the new Chapel. On arriving at Dunstan I had dinner with George Dodds and Mr. and Mrs. Coulson, and after dinner we all went to Rowlands Gill and were present at the stone laying. Later in the evening, a tea and public meeting was held in a large marquee, but we saw no more of my brother and his wife who had returned home on account of the railway timetable having been altered. While we were at Rowlands railway station, I met Mr. and Mrs. Fred Farmiloe. I have previously seen Mr. Farmiloe, and was only slightly acquainted with his wife, but we were soon chatting as familiarly as though we had known each

CHAPTER 3

other from childhood. Mr. Farmiloe is clerk at the large flour mill at Dunstan, where his father is manager. After leaving the train we walked to Dunstan, where I spent the night.

Tuesday August 6th (14th day).

Had a long talk with by brother in his office at Gateshead, when we drew up a circular and syllabus of lectures that I hope to deliver while in England, and afterwards we came to Newcastle, where we looked at some lanterns at Watsons in Granger Street. We made no final selection but intend to call again on Thursday. In the afternoon Mrs. Dodds and I visited Elswick cemetery where our dear little Willie[59], and the late Mr. George Dodds, lie peacefully at rest till the trumpet shall sound and mortality be swallowed up of life. My sister and I each laid flowers on the beds of our dear ones. Mr. Dodds entered into rest on April 1st 1901, and our dear little Willie on September 30th, 1869.

Wednesday August 7th (15th day).

This morning I wrote several letters and in the afternoon Mrs. Dodds, Miss. Ella Wilson, my nephew Bert and myself drove out to Ponteland. It is difficult to describe my feelings as we drove along the well-remembered road, every inch of which I had travelled scores of times.[60] Every hill and hollow, every house and almost every tree by the roadside

---

[59] Thomas's son, who was born and died in 1869.

[60] He is approaching Ponteland from Newcastle, which lies to the south east. His route is the present-day B6918.

seemed to be like meeting an old friend. A new house or two, the removal of a tollgate, a belt of young trees along the moor edge, were the principal alterations I have noticed.

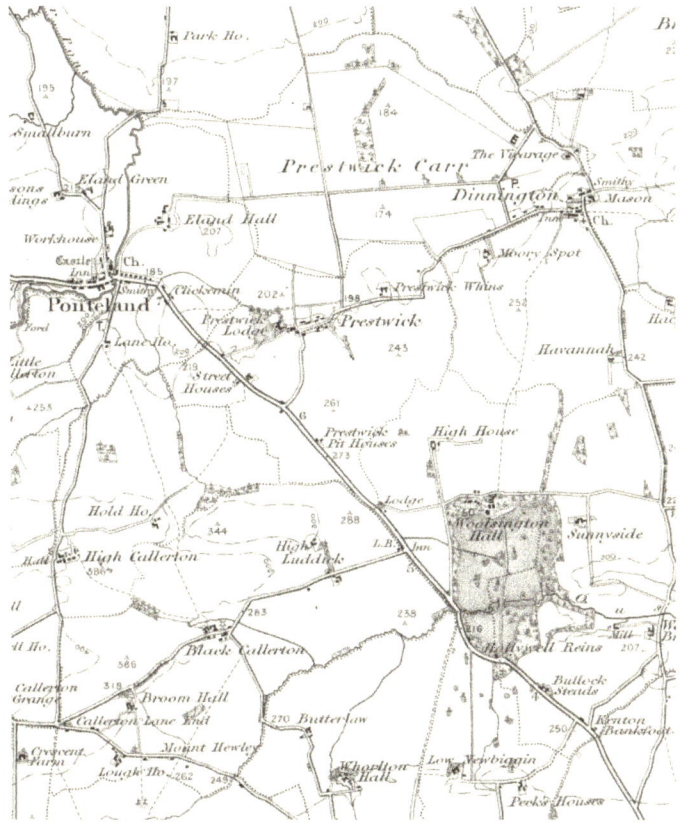

Figure 39 The south east of Ponteland. The map is about four miles wide. (Ordnance Survey 1" map from 1896, David Rumsey collection, reproduced with permission).

We pulled up before reaching Kenton Bank Foot[61] where I had served my apprenticeship. The premises are now occupied by Mr. Wm Jameson and I wondered if they would

---

[61] South east corner of the map, Figure 39.

CHAPTER 3

know me after so long an absence, so I walked up to the door a little ahead of my travelling companions, and in answer to my knock the door was opened by Mrs. Jameson, who for some time seemed unable to comprehend the situation, but when she recognized the personality of their visitor he and his friends were cordially invited to stay for refreshments, which were reluctantly declined, we being anxious to get to the end of our journey as soon as possible.

So on we went, past the blacksmith's shop, past Bullock Steads, Woolsington Lodge with its well remembered chain-fence and wide approach to the lodge gate, past Woolsington Bridge, the Wheat Sheaf Inn, Prestwick Pit Houses, the Street House and up to the Round Hill Gate, where we got the first view of "Our Mecca." On arriving at Clickemin Bridge I got out of the trap, preferring to walk up Bell Villas, so that I might the more leisurely take in the old familiar scene.

The first old acquaintance I saw was Mr. John Jameson (Figure 40). He and I were playmates in boyhood, we were members of the Church of England choir, the village quadrille party, and later both became members of the Methodist Church, and in many other ways our interests were identical up to the time I left for New Zealand.

VISITING ENGLAND IN 1901

Figure 40 Thomas's friend John Jameson and his wife Annie *circa* **1890. (Photographer: unknown, Ponteland Local History Society Archives, reproduced with permission).**

I failed to recognize him at first, but in a few minutes his features became familiar in spite of altered appearance. I then went to his place of business, intending to give Mrs. Jameson a surprise. I have known her as long as I have known her husband and did not think she would know me, but I was mistaken.

Chapter 3

I had calculated on springing a series of little surprises on my old friends, but after my experience since I arrived in the North of England, and especially today, I no longer entertain the idea. Whether from memory or intuition I don't know, but somehow or other I seemed to be known by all those to whom I spoke, and my arrival was soon known throughout the village, and I no longer tried to disguise my identity.

I went up the village and had a long walk with my father's youngest brother[62] who is still living in the same house as when I left for New Zealand. In fact it is the only house in which he and his wife have lived since they married; in fact it is the house in which his late wife[63] was born, lived and died. On entering I was struck with the fact that the furniture stood in the same position as I remember it to have done when I was a lad: bed, couch, tables, grandfather clock, chest of drawers, cases of stuffed birds, all as I remembered them fifty years ago.

We called on Mr. James Stobert who lives a little higher up the village, where I also met his son Henry, and also his daughter Hannah, now Mrs. Meek. I was able to recognize both though mere children when I saw them last. Martin and Mrs. Jameson who live on the opposite side to the street, were intimate friends of mine long before I went to Newcastle, and I hurried across the road hoping to see them, but was sorry to learn Mr. Jameson were not at home, but I had the pleasure of having half an hour's chat with Mrs Jameson and their daughter.

---

[62] William Laws.

[63] Ann Oliver.

VISITING ENGLAND IN 1901

I had a look at "Pont-side", and crossed the steps leading to Van Diemen's Land[64] and the gardens on the opposite side of the river, then into the Seven Stars Inn, took a general survey of the old brewery and other buildings, everything being of the deepest interest, even down to the fowl houses, the pig stys, and the old pump. I had a look at the building that was formerly a day school kept by Mr Ralph Brown and which was the only day school I ever went to, but the building is a school no longer, but being now used as a stable and I went in and had a look at the horses.

The Seven Stars Inn was kept by Mrs. Yeaman who was my mother's aunt[65], and with whom I lived from the time I was a year and nine months old, until I was through my apprenticeship at 21 years of age.[66]

The village church is where three generations of my forefathers sleep, the little chapel where I first went to Sunday school, and the little chapel that I attended and in which I frequently preached. I had a cup of tea, before I left, with Mr. and Mrs. John Jameson and got away at 7:30 and reached The Crescent at 10 p.m.

---

[64] Presumably it was named after the real Van Diemen's Land.

[65] She was actually his father's aunt.

[66] An apprenticeship usually lasted seven years, so Thomas must have left school at the age of fourteen.

CHAPTER 3

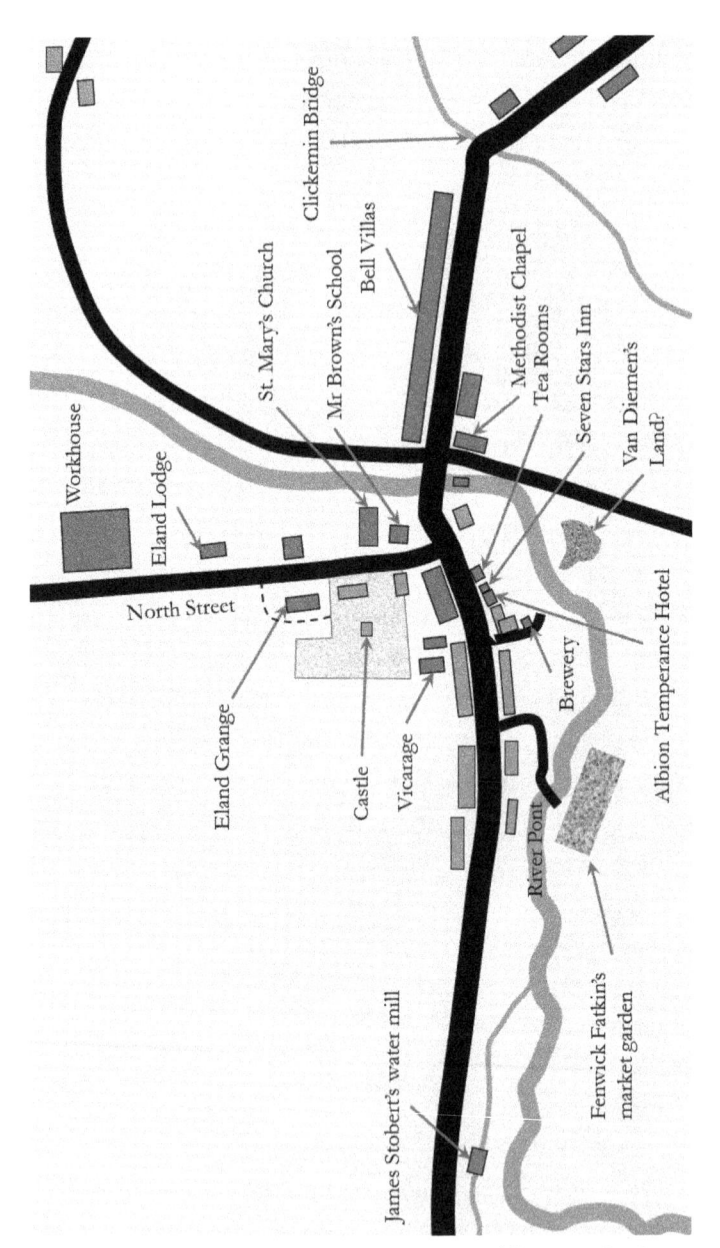

Figure 41 Sketch map of Ponteland in 1901. The map is about ½ mile wide. (Drawn by Robert Laws).

Thursday August 8th (16th day).

Met my brother by appointment this morning, and then went to Watson's in Granger Street, where I purchased a lantern, and other accessories costing £8.3.0. We then took the train for Ulsworth where the trap was waiting to take us up to Washington. There were present: Jack and Mary, Mr. and Mrs. Dickinson, Helen, Monty, Con, Norman[67], and we spent a delightful evening. I have neglected to include the name of Gertie[68], who was also present. Helen presided at the piano and we had singing both sacred and secular and my brother's singing of "Mr. McArthy" will live in the memory of the audience for years to come. I see I have omitted to note another song of my brother's which also brought down the house: that was "The Ship that Brought Me Over." I will never forget these two songs.

Friday August 9th (17th day).

Spent the day Washington. Wrote to The Rev. C. E. Beecroft and spent some time in conversation with Mr. Dickinson, who is an old resident here and knew with whom I was acquainted when I lived in Eighton Banks in 1863–1864.

My brother came home in the afternoon, and we had a pleasant walk as far as the river Wear; we passed through some fine pastures, and also through fields of wheat and oats

---

[67] Helen, Monty, Con, and Norman are Jack's children by his first wife, Barbara.

[68] It is not known who Gertie was.

Chapter 3

now ready for the sickle. Our prime topic of conversation was the Boer war, on which we took opposite sides he contending the British were the aggressors and the Boers deserved our sympathy, while I took on an entirely opposite view.

We got home at 8 p.m. and spent another pleasant evening.

Saturday August 10th (18th day).

Jack and I came from Washington this morning and on arriving at the central station he went to his office and I to The Crescent, and after lunch my sister and I took a cab and went out to Ponteland where we hope to spend a week. We had secured lodgings with Mrs. Mackey, near the centre of the village, where we arrived and took possession about noon. Mr. John Jameson had asked me to sleep at his house, and on account of our intimacy in former years his kind offer was gladly accepted.

Shortly after leaving the Bank Foot we were caught in a thunder storm, we inside the cab were dry and comfortable, and I am sorry to say, and have been ever since, that I did not think of asking the driver to shelter with us and share our comfort.

At 6 o'clock we arrived at the village and had a stroll up the village, and called upon my dear old uncle Willie. Mr. and Mrs. Martin Jameson, who I am happy to say continues to be strong and vigorous.

VISITING ENGLAND IN 1901

Figure 42 New Zealand troops marching down Wellesley Street, Auckland, to embark for the Boer War in 1901. (Sir George Grey Special Collections, Auckland Libraries, item AWNS-19010208-5-1, originally published by the Auckland Weekly News, from Wikipedia).

Sunday August 11th (19th day).

Went to the Sunday school where I took a class and gave a short address. I gave my first address here in 1860, and it seemed strange that, after all those years, I should stand once more in the dear old place. The teachers then, so far as I remember, were James Stobert, Superintendent, George Weddell, John Reary, and myself. Miss. Weddell, who was then a teacher, is now married and living at Wallbottle. John Reary is now a Wesleyan minister in Newfoundland, and I

CHAPTER 3

am a local preacher in New Zealand, Mr. Stobert being still superintendent.

Figure 43 The Langtons outside the vicarage in Ponteland. (Photographer: unknown, Ponteland Local History Society Archives, reproduced with permission).

At 10.30, I went to the Anglican Church, where the vicar, the Rev. F. W. Langton (Figure 43) preached. At 2.30 p.m. I went again to the old chapel, where a local preacher named Turnbull conducted the service, and in the evening I had the pleasure of once more occupying the pulpit.

Monday August 12th (20th day).

Spent most of the day in looking up old friends of whom I found a good number, among whom were James Stobert, his son Henry, and his daughter Hannah, the two latter being children when I left for New Zealand, John and Mrs. Jameson, Martin Jameson and his wife, James Jameson, John Edward and Mrs. Temperley, Mrs Stewart, and no doubt others of whom memory fails.

After lunch my sister and I had a walk up the North Lane[69] past the Anglican church, and past the house on the opposite side in which my father and mother lived not long after their marriage and in which my sister Susan was born and died at the age of 3½ years[70]. On we went, past the workhouse[71], and when we got to Eland Green we surveyed the cottage in which I first saw the light. To this house, I see another storey has been added since I saw it last. My brother Jack cycled out during the afternoon, and together we surveyed the home of our boyhood.

One of the most pleasing incidents to me, was the finding of a nail I had driven into the wall of a building at Eland Green when I would be about seven or eight years of age. Over its hiding place I had carved, in the soft stone with my hammer and stout nail, the letters "T.L.P." thus representing my name and birthplace.[72] It was some time before I was able to find the work of former years, but at length Jack

---

[69] North Lane is called North Road on modern maps.

[70] Susan (Susannah 1st) was born on 4 June, 1842 and died on 12 January 1846 of scarlet fever. She is buried in the graveyard at Ponteland.

[71] The workhouse stood on what is now Guardians Court.

[72] The letters 'T.L.P.' are still visible today. They are on the north-facing wall of the cottage shown in Figure 44, about 3 feet above the ground.

Chapter 3

discovered them a great deal lower in the wall than where I had been looking, forgetting that I have grown considerably during the intervening years.

Figure 44 A cottage at Eland Green, where Thomas might have been born. (Photographer: Clare Stephenson, reproduced with permission).

Tuesday August 13th (21st day).

Today my sister and I surveyed the gardens formerly in possession of my aunt[73], again I found myself at a loss to explain by pen and ink all I would like to say. There stood the old Green Jack pear tree, from which I had gathered the

---

[73] He means his great aunt, Mrs Yeaman, who brought him up.

Visiting England in 1901

fruit and filled my pockets times without number. The tree seems today just as I remember it in years gone by. Some of the fruit had fallen, and the wasps were regaling themselves as in the days long of long ago. Several of the old apple trees were still standing. The Mount and Keswick Codlings, and the "Polly" were still looking strong and healthy, in their green old age.

Later in the day we were shown through the Seven Stars Hotel, by Mr. Hogg who was then the landlord. I had a lively re-collection of every nook and corner. The stone flagged passage and back kitchen, with the long settle[74] down one side and the spirit bar in one corner. The kitchen was on the left of the passage and was really the living room of the house, and here the business of the Inn was carried on. On the opposite side of the passage was the tap room, here travellers on business met their customers, and transacted business they had to do. The principle and the largest room in the house was the dining room, here public meetings and public dinners were held, and as a matter of course, it was the largest and the best furnished room in the house, the size of this room was 24 feet by 12 feet. Also there was a small room known as "the bar" though never used for that purpose, it was generally used as a spare room in which the girls did their sewing or entertaining their friends. There was still the little cupboard where my aunt kept her stock of long pipes or "churchwardens" and another little cupboard where she kept her stock of jellies.

---

[74] A 'settle' was a long wooden seat with back and arms, and usually with storage space inside.

CHAPTER 3

We went upstairs and through the bedrooms, the one of most interest being the one I occupied for several years during the last three or four years I was at school. We then went up another flight of stairs that communicated with what was termed "the long room" and ran the full length of that part of the house, which was for when balls, public meetings and entertainments were held. It was here we met for weekly string band practice every Saturday evening and after this, for about half an hour, we had a little social dance or quadrille party. This has been a memorable day, but the half has not been told.

Wednesday August 14th (22nd day).

This morning my sister and I walked up the village as far as the water-mill, where Mr. Stobert grinds his flour, and in the afternoon we walked out as far as Smallburn and had tea with Mr. and Mrs. Humphrey Atkinson. Mr. Atkinson was a member of the Methodist Church at Bell's Close and he and I were shopmates at the Elswick Ordinance Works[75], Newcastle, and also at St. Peter's shipyard Newcastle.

In the evening we took our way up Callerton Lane as far as Dunn's Green, and passed many a well-known spot on our way, and on our way back we called at the Lane House and made enquiry for the son who at one time resided with his parents, but were told he had gone down to Ponteland so we failed to see him. I remember him as one of the most promising Sabbath Scholars, but was told in the village later

---

[75] The factory built by Lord William Armstrong who developed the rifled artillery barrel and the breach loading of shells.

VISITING ENGLAND IN 1901

in the evening that he had given way to drink, that he had drifted far from the right path and had lost the respect of his former friends.

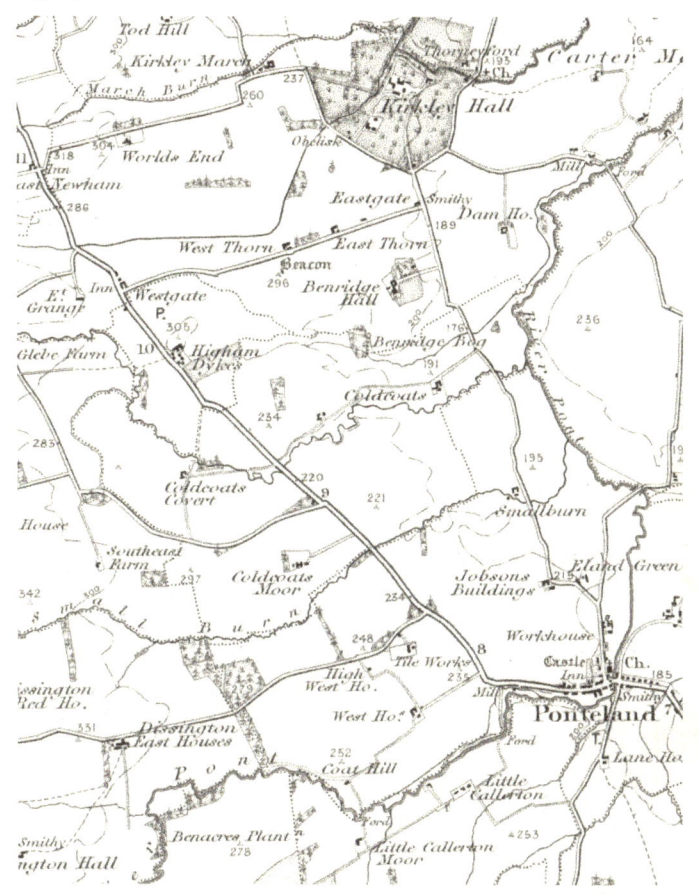

Figure 45 The north west of Ponteland. The map is about three miles wide. (Ordnance Survey 1" map from 1896, David Rumsey collection, reproduced with permission).

CHAPTER 3

Thursday August 15th (23rd day).

Went down to the little river Pont this morning by the way of the church yard fence, and came across the following curious notice:

> Any person throwing or tipping, or permitting to be thrown or tipped, or to fall into the river Pont, any stones, ashes, refuse, filth, or dead animals, or birds, or causing to be permitted to flow, or pass there into, any solid or liquid sewage, or refuse matter will be prosecuted.
>
> By order of the Local Board
> Geo Williamson
> Clerk

Later in the day Mr. W. Jameson took me to Kenton Bank Foot, where we had lunch, and in the afternoon we drove to Westerhope, where we saw some well-kept gardens and some beautiful tomatoes, and after supper we returned to Ponteland about 11 p.m. Before starting out this morning I had a long talk with an old gentleman named Meek[76], who knew my dear father and spoke very highly of him.

Friday August 16th (24th day).

Spent the forenoon in looking around the village, and after lunch my sister and I went to Dissington Tile Sheds. Mr. Bowning had very kindly put his horse and trap at our disposable, and taking advantage of his offer we had a fine

---

[76] The Meek family still farm at Eland Hall Farm.

drive around the district. Our route lay by way of Higham Dykes, The Waggon[77], The Highlander, The World's End (Kirkley West Farm), Kirkley Cottages, Benridge and Eland Hall, Ponteland.

Let me here say a word or two about the places I have named. Highham Dykes is a large country residence, kept by an old fashioned lady named Miss. Bell. She was widely known for her benevolence, and treated her retainers as though they were members of her family. She, in the company with a lady who lived with her at the house, drove every Sunday to Ponteland church in a tandem drawn by two donkeys.

"The Waggon" was the sign of a public house that stood about 200 yards West of Higham Dykes. This is the name of the hamlet, where Miss Bell lives and has lived ever since 1850. "The Highlander", another public house, lay about a mile beyond the Waggon. I should think, judging for the position they occupied, that little business would be done at either house.

The World's End, or Kirkley West Farm, was occupied and farmed by my father for about seven years[78], it is only poor land I am told, and my poor father got little out of it, but I generally came from Ponteland and spent the Harvest holidays here and, though 50 years have elapsed, I shall remember the position of the farm buildings and fields, and

---

[77] This is spelled 'Wagon' on the 1896 map, but 'Waggon' on modern maps.

[78] It is not clear when Thomas's father farmed at World's End.

Chapter 3

even the position of the gates by the roadside, with many other things that I need not mention here.

Kirkley Cottages consists of four small houses, they are a short distance from Kirkley Hall, the seat or home of the Ogle family. At this time my father's sister, her husband and family live in the cottage at the north end of the row, and my cousin Tom and his wife and only daughter live in the house at the south end.

Benridge, like Higham Dykes is a little hamlet clustered around a fine large residence, or Hall, in which a gentleman named Blackett lives with his family and a number of retainers. Eland Green is the name of a farm situated about three quarters of a mile distant from Ponteland. The residential quarters consists of two large, but old-fashioned, comfortable farm houses, and about a dozen little cottages in which live the people who find employment nearby, and one in which I happened to be born.

On arriving at the Tile Sheds we had tea with the Bowrings and after spending the evening with them Mr. Bowring took us to Ponteland in his trap, and as Mr. Jameson was just leaving for Newcastle, he prevailed upon my sister and me to accompany him. The drive today was most enjoyable, the associations were delightful, the country was dressed in its best, the weather was beautiful, and the conversation agreeable. Let me now say that both on behalf of my sister and myself that our week at Ponteland has been a time of great delight.

Saturday August 17th (25th day).

Left Ponteland and walked as far as Kenton Bank Foot on my way to Newcastle. This time I did not find a nail I had driven into the wall near the Wheat Sheaf Inn[79] when I was an apprentice. I had seen it hundreds of times when passing to and fro, but it has now vanished probably having been destroyed by the rust of the last thirty years. Had I found it I would have taken it with me to New Zealand and given it a place among my treasures.

I had arranged to wait for my sister at the Bank Foot, but as Mr. Jameson was just leaving for Newcastle he prevailed upon me to ride with him, and we arrived in town about 2 p.m., my sister coming on in Mr. Bowring's trap and getting to town an hour later. The week at Ponteland had proved one of unalloyed pleasure, "a season of grace and sweet delight." Many a time from distant New Zealand I have turned my longing eyes in this direction, but the pleasure of anticipation has been eclipsed by the pleasure of realization.

Sunday August 18th (26th day).

Wrote letter to Mrs. Laws and Charlie and did not attend church until the evening, when I went to Elswick Road, where I heard Mr. Thompson Walton preach a good sermon

---

[79] The Wheat Sheaf Inn was located at the present-day Callerton roundabout on the B6918, 2¾ miles south east of Ponteland.

CHAPTER 3

from the words "Jesus only." Mr. Walton was a scavenger[80] in Newcastle, and is now employed in some colliery in the district. A prayer meeting was held at the conclusion of the service and I was pleased to see Sir Wm Stephenson go forward to take his stand by Mr. Walton's side.

Monday Aug 19th (27th day).

Went to South Shields this morning by boat, and was struck with the improvements that have taken place since I left England. There is now an endless succession of houses, factories, shipyards, warehouses, etc. from the Swing Bridge, to Tynemouth. Ship building seems to be going on briskly.

Eight new torpedo destroyers were either in the water or on the stocks at Palmers Yard, and the *Russell* – the first battleship launched during King Edward's reign – had come off the slips yesterday. But I was as much interested in the *Turbinia*[81] as in anything I saw. It will be remembered that

---

[80] A 'scavenger' made his meagre living by searching for lumps of unburnt coal in the ash collected from local houses.

[81] The *Turbinia* was built by Charles Parsons and was propelled by his newly invented steam turbine. Parsons had not managed to persuade the Royal Navy of the value of his invention so he gate-crashed the Naval review at Spithead. Queen Victoria looked on as *Turbinia* wove between the lines of warships and out-ran the Navy's fastest cutters. By doing this, Parsons forced the authorities to take the new propulsion system seriously. The Queen was sufficiently amused that she commissioned a painting of the event. The *Turbinia* can be seen in the Discovery Museum in central Newcastle.

this little boat attracted a great deal of attention during the recent review at Spithead on the occasion of Her Majesty's Jubilee in 1897.

Figure 46 The *Turbinia* in 1897 travelling at 34 knots. (Photographer: Alfred John West 1857–1937, Tyne and Wear Archives and Museums, from Wikipedia).

From the steamboat landing we steamed to Tynemouth, where Bert called on Mr. Buckley, one of the members of his choir, and after a few minutes' stay we started on our return journey and got to my sister's at The Crescent in time for tea.

Tuesday August 20th (28th day).

Had a wire from Bainbridge, asking me to spend the weekend with him at Saltersgate and to take the services on the Sunday so I went to his place of business in Market St. and told him I would agree to his suggestion and obtained

CHAPTER 3

further instructions from the expert who met me on a former occasion. Here we tried the lantern and everything appeared to work satisfactorily, though the test was not concluded as I was leaving for Edinburgh at 3.35.

I then left as just stated and got to my destination at 6.30. I have no difficulty in finding Mr. Brydone, who is living with his niece, Mrs. Kelly. Mr. Brydone came to Napier about 1873 and at once identified himself with Trinity Church, and in this way we became friends. In 1895 Mrs. Brydone died and her husband returned to England, where he lived a few years and finally settled in Edinburgh, where he died June 4th, 1905.[82]

Wednesday August 21st (29th day).

Took a walk round the Grange this morning, and in the afternoon Mr. Brydon, Mrs. Kelly and I went to Leith by the little steamer *Scotsman*. From the deck of the boat we viewed the Forth Bridge from several angles. The erection of workshops began in 1883 and the foundation of the bridge began also on 1883 and from this period till January 1890 the work went on to completion. Three days afterwards, the first train passed over. The time taken to build the bridge was seven years, and the number of workmen employed was 4000. More than 500 accidents occurred during its erection, 57 ending fatally. The length of the cantilevers is 350 feet, and the height of the railway above high water mark 89 feet, the weight of iron and steel used, about 54,000 tons. The

---

[82] These words were added in about 1931.

total length of the bridge is about a mile and a half, and the cost close on 3¼ millions sterling.

I may briefly mention Aberdour and Queensferry. The first is a pleasant village on the Fife coast, and is about six miles from Leith, and is a pleasant resort for the people of Edinburgh. Queensferry is a very old town and rich in antiquarian lore. I noticed an old house on which was cut on the lintel over the doorway "SPES MEA CHRISTVS S.W.A.P. 1641."[83]

We also went through the church of St. Margaret, formerly a Carmelite monastery, and said to be the oldest church in Scotland, and dates from the 12th century, and is reported to be the burying place of the Dundas family, and there are several tablets erected to various members of this family.

I was pleased to see the following request, framed and hung in this old church.

> Whosoever thou art who entereth this church, leave it not without prayer to God for thyself, and for those who minister and for those who worship here.

We drove to the Grange by way of Dalmeny – the seat of Lord Roseberry (but did not wait upon his Lordship) – and got to Edinburgh at 6.30. After tea, Mr. Brydone and I called on Mrs. Donald and her daughter, Mrs. Smalley, the latter being the wife of the late Rev. J. S. Smalley, who was

---

[83] This is the famous Doorway to Plewlands. The house was built for the couple Samuel Wilson and Anna Ponton (S.W.A.P.).

CHAPTER 3

appointed the first Wesleyan minister to the town in Napier, New Zealand in 1874, and later in the evening Mrs. Kelly piloted me to Viewforth, where I spent the remainder of the evening with my cousin, Mrs. Cowell, who is now a widow living with her married daughter.

Thursday August 22nd (30th day).

Took the 10 a.m. train for Glasgow, and had a day at the Exhibition,[84] but it would have taken a month to properly examine all I saw, but I made the most of the time at my disposal.

Figure 47 Letterhead of the Glasgow International Exhibition, 1901. (Designer: John Brown, Collectie Roermond Cuypershuis, Netherlands, from Wikipedia).

---

[84] The Glasgow International Exhibition ran between 2 May and 4 November, 1901.

I hurried through the Canadian, Queensland, and Australian courts, and did the same with the Japanese, French, Persian and other courts, and the same may be said of the machinery, statuary, pictures and other sections. I also had a peep at the water-chute, switchback railway; listened to the Russian, and British, military, and regimental bands, and got back to Edinburgh at 6.30, surfeited but not satisfied. I had tried to grasp too much with so small a hand. I returned to Edinburgh about 6.30.

Friday August 23rd (31st day).

Early this morning, my nephew – Mr. Bert Dodds, and a friend of his named Steward, arrived from Newcastle, and after having a little refreshment we went to Carlton Hill, and saw the monuments erected to the memory of Robert Burns, Lord Nelson, Dugald Steward, and probably others, also the unfinished memorial of what is known as "Edinburgh's Folly." We also took note of Arthur's Seat, and Salisbury Crag.

We then returned to Hatton Place for lunch, which included a real Scotch haggis which we Englishmen unanimously pronounced to be first class. Bert, Steward, and I then set off for Waverley station, where I got the 2.50 train for Newcastle and arrived at 6.50 p.m. My nephew and his friend intended to leave for Newcastle at 6 p.m., which they probably did. My wife and I were in Edinburgh in 1869 and much that we saw then I remembered today.

CHAPTER 3

Saturday August 24th (32nd day).

Spent most of the day at The Crescent preparing for services at Saltersgate Tomorrow. At 5.25 p.m. I caught the train for Blackhill, where Mr. Bainbridge met me, and we drove to his shooting-box at Saltersgate where we arrived about 7 p.m. The place is moorland as far as the eye can reach and the physical features not unlike some of the broken country in New Zealand. Mr. Bainbridge and I had a long walk together and talked of many things that were of mutual interest. I find him to be the same kind, genial Christian gentleman, as in former years. He is one of the few I have known, whose character has not been spoiled by the acquisition of wealth. After our return, we had dinner, then family prayer, a general conversation, and then we retired for the night.

Sunday August 25th (33rd day).

Preached twice at Saltersgate. In the morning I had a fair amount of liberty, but in the evening I had an unhappy time, and felt as though hammering against a brick wall, and that what I was saying did not reach the congregation. Except for this experience I had a happy time at Saltersgate.

In the afternoon my host drove a short distance to see his mother, and during his absence I had a quiet stroll through the woods and home by way of the moor, and the heather being in full bloom added to my enjoyment. We had another long walk later in the evening, and again indulged in reminiscences of bygone days, and although socially he and I are wide as the poles asunder there was an entire absence of reserve between us.

Monday August 26th (34th day).

Journeyed to Newcastle in company with Mr. and Mrs. Bainbridge and family, and on arriving at the Central station I booked for Spennymoor in order to spend a few hours with my wife's sister and her husband, Mr. and Mrs. Dees and family. Her husband, who formerly was a Congregational minister, resigned because he could hardly live on the small stipend he received. He is now cashier at a large ironworks at Spennymoor. They have a family of ten children and I found them happy and comfortable. He still preaches for the Congregational and other denominations when his services are required. I left by the 8.20 p.m., which left us too little time for all we would liked to have said about past events, though that subject had a good deal of our attention.

I learned a good deal about the last days of my wife's father and mother, and about the old times at Cottenham Street, also about her brother Jack[85], her sisters Betsy – now Mrs. Liddell. Sallie remains unmarried and is now in South Africa, Lucy – now married and living in Blenheim, New Zealand, and her brothers, Tom and William, both living in Australia, Tom in Melbourne and William at Castlemaine, Victoria.

---

[85] Not to be confused with Thomas's brother, also called Jack.

CHAPTER 3

Tuesday August 27th (35th day).

Spent the day at The Crescent where I and my sister met with an old friend in the person of Miss. Annie Cooper who is now a widow, who is visiting a friend at Newcastle. My late wife and Miss. Cooper were great chums in the now distant old Blenheim Street days, which were just about the time I came to work in Newcastle and I only have a hazy remembrance of their names, which have frequently been mentioned in conversation. Later in the afternoon I went to Elswick Cemetery, where here again I saw the grassy beds in which our dear little Willie, and my brother in law Mr. George Dodds, peacefully sleep.

Wednesday August 28th (36th day).

Wrote several letters and afterwards took a stroll in Elswick Park. The ground formerly belonged to Mr. Christian Alshusen, and was about to be sold for building allotments when a few public gentlemen, whose names I could not discover, purchased the Hall and ground, and held them until purchased by the council. The grounds are nicely laid out, and are visited by a large number of townsfolk and visitors from a distance, and the principal works of the sculptors Lough and Noble are housed in the Hall.

In the afternoon I went to town and made a few purchases, and on my way home called on Mr. and Mrs. W. Plews. I was slightly acquainted with Mrs. Plews before I left England. She is a daughter of Mrs. Thomas Reary of Ponteland, and a sister of the Rev. John Reary now a

Wesleyan Minister in Newfoundland. I spent a couple of pleasant hours with my old friends at Bude Street. My sister, Mrs. George Dodds, went to Harrogate on a brief visit to the Rev. and Mrs. Rhodes, and got home about 11.30 p.m.

Thursday August 29th (37th day).

Went to Whitley this afternoon and called on Mr. and Mrs. John Newlands. Mr. Newlands is my late dear wife's youngest brother, who was formerly a glass-stainer in Newcastle. They live in property of their own at North Parade, and let apartments. After coming home I went to the Tynemouth Palace – formerly "The Aquarium" – where my nephew, Mr George Dodds, gave an organ recital. I was very desirous to hear him as he is reported to be one of the most accomplished musicians in the North of England.[86] I hope and believe that he maintained his reputation, but I am no judge in such matters. The Ladies' Band was very good, the Fair Fountain, beautiful, and the rest of the entertainment did not interest me a great deal.

Friday August 30th (38th day).

I have no record of this day's proceedings.

---

[86] George Dodds's book 'Voice Placing and Training Exercises' was published in 1929, and it is still in print.

CHAPTER 3

Saturday August 31st (39th day).

Spent most of the morning in trying to see The Rev. A. B. Jebb for whom I have a letter of introduction from Mr. James Trevor. Mr. Jebb is not only a minister of the Gospel, but is also in business and has an office on the Sandhill. This is the third time I have called, and I failed to see him each time. I then went over to Gateshead hoping to find my brother Jack who, I was told, was doing business at the North Shields.

On my return to Newcastle, I had lunch at Lockhart's Cocoa Rooms, and then went to Mr. Winter, Optician, where I have my sight tested and ordered a pair of dual focus glasses. After this I had a look through the corn market thinking I might meet my friend, Mr. Stobert, but learned he was not in town.

While in the market I met Mr. Tom Richardson, who was one of our local preachers whom I knew very well before I left England. I never doubted that he would remember me, but was surprised to find that he had no recollection of me whatever, not even my family name though my people were all adherents of the Wesleyan Methodist Church and had attended the village chapel for many years and had often listened to his preaching.

I fear he took me to be one of those imposters who worm themselves into the confidence of their dupes, and after having fleeced them, leave them to ruminate on their own stupidity. But Mr. Richardson took good care that he would have no folly of this kind to morn over. I could not help contrasting the kindness and hospitality I had received from Mr. Tom Bainbridge with the icy indifference I got from Mr. Tom Richardson.

Sunday September 1st (40th day).

This morning I heard the Rev. Dr. Watkins in The People's Hall, Rye Hill, on the subject of Church Praise and the discourse was deeply impressive, and after the service I went to Dunstan and had lunch with my sister and her husband, Mr. and Mrs. Coulthard. In the afternoon my brother conducted a thanks giving service in Dunstan Chapel, and in the evening we all went to Bensham Road, where The Rev. Mark Guy-Pearce preached one of his characteristic services "Take no thought for the morrow", or as he put it "Don't Worry." At the close of the service I had a few moments with the preacher when I reminded him that I had the pleasure of taking tea with him in the Napier Parsonage during the ministry of the Rev. Edward Best.

Monday September 2nd (41st day).

Spent the day with Mrs. Coulthard at Dunstan and in the evening Mrs. Dodds came over from Newcastle. I then met Jack at his office. We then went to Hewitt's photographic establishment in Catherine Terrace where we had a group photo taken, and also one of myself at their request, for family distribution.

In the evening we heard the Rev. Guy Pearce lecture in Bensham Road Chapel on "West Country Worthies." I will not attempt to describe the lecture, but it was worthy of the man. After the Lecture I met Mr. George Rowell of

CHAPTER 3

Kibblesworth, whose acquaintance I made before I left England, and in those days I generally had a quarterly appointment at Kibblesworth and after a little talk with my old friend he left for his home, and the rest of the party returned to Dunstan, where we chatted till midnight.

Tuesday September 3rd (42nd day).

After having lunch at Dunstan I went to The Crescent, and in the afternoon I wrote to Mr. James Stobert, and to Mr. T. H. Bainbridge, and in the evening my brother Jack came along and we met the expert from Watson's, who gave the lantern a thorough testing to our complete satisfaction, and handed it over to us. My brother went home by a late train. I owe him a deep debt of gratitude for the many sacrifices he has made on my behalf, and for the loving interest he has taken in all my proceedings since coming to England.

Wednesday September 4th (43rd day).

Wrote to Mr. R. Ashcroft and Mr. W. Blackmore, and afterwards to no 10 Dunstan Terrace, where my youngest sister resides, and here spent the afternoon and had tea. I had arranged to meet Jack at the office at 5 p.m. for I had seen so little of my sister since I came north, and we had so many things to talk over. Jack however, was wise enough to go home and I followed by train, leaving Gateshead at 8 p.m. and it was after 9 p.m. before I got to my brother's. When I was in the Gateshead Circuit I often preached at Washington, and would have liked to see the chapel again, but unfortunately none of those I had spoken to could tell me where it had stood.

Thursday September 5th (44th day).

Took a quiet stroll through the village this morning, and later prepared an address I am to give at Dunstan next Sunday, when I am to take the chair at the Harvest Thanksgiving service. Jack came home about 4.30, and Mrs. Gibson, a friend of his from Manchester, arrived shortly after at the request of my sister-in-law – Mrs. R. C. Laws of Napier. I called on her cousin, Mr. Turnbull, with whom I had a long conversation on family matters, which I hope to report to his sister if I am spared to reach Napier. Mr. Gibson is a Wesleyan and a lover of music, so we spent a delightful evening singing the old Methodist hymns and also others of more recent date.

Friday September 6th (45th day).

Spent the morning at Washington preparing for the service at Dunstan on Sunday afternoon. Left Washington at 1.30 for Ulsworth where I was interviewed by a representative of the "Leader", one of the Newcastle papers[87]. His enquires were generally either in the direction of commerce or politics, and on those subjects I could give him only second-hand information. Had the information been more on New Zealand lines such as Scenery, the natives, Hot Lake District, climate and kindred subjects, he

---

[87] The Newcastle Daily Leader. It ceased publication in 1903.

CHAPTER 3

would have got more interesting information, both as regards quality and quantity.

After having a cup of tea with my brother, I went to The Crescent and found a letter from The Rev. F. W. Langton vicar of Ponteland, saying that I was expected to lecture there on Monday next.

News is published today of the attempted[88] assassination of President McKinley.

Saturday September 7th (46th day).

Went to town this morning to arrange about sending my lantern to Ponteland for my lecture on Monday next, and was fortunate in finding a native of the village and also a carrier who was pleased to undertake the job and I addressed it care of Mr. John Jameson. After tea at Lockhart's I returned to The Crescent and spent a pleasant evening with my dear sister Mrs. ['Sallie'] Dodds. Bert had a run on his bike as far as Ponteland this afternoon.

Sunday September 8th (47th day).

Stayed at home this morning, preparing for the Harvest Home at Dunstan. Sallie and I went over after lunch and at the appointed time I have a 15 minutes' address, and took the chair. The title of the cantata is "The Harvest Home in the temple days", and the service went without a hitch. We had tea at Coulthards and then came to Elswick Road Chapel where one the Houghton-le-Spring ministers

---

[88] He died from his wounds on 14 September 1901.

preached from Luke XXIII. 42 "Lord remember me when thou comest into thy Kingdom." Both sermon and singing were good.

Monday September 9th (48th day).

Walked to Ponteland and had lunch at Jameson's, Kenton Bank Foot, on the way. After, Mr. Jameson's son Edward went with me to the schoolroom and helped me to fix the lantern at 7.30. The Rev. Mr. Brash was preaching in the Methodist Church, and very kindly began the service half an hour earlier in order that the congregation might attend the lecture.

My nephew Bert manipulated the lantern most successfully, and I had the satisfaction of speaking to a crowded audience. I might have cut the lecture a little shorter with advantage, and exhibited about 60 slides instead of 80. I have been requested to lecture again on Thursday next on our mineral Resources; Trade and Commerce; The Land Question; and The Government. Proceeds of the lecture £2.7.9. Bert cycled back to Newcastle at the conclusion of the lecture.

Tuesday September 10th (49th day).

Spent the forenoon at Ponteland in having another ramble about the old place. Saw my uncle Willie and afterwards had lunch with Mr. and Mrs. John Jameson. I then walked to Newcastle[89], in order to select my slides for

---

[89] A distance of 7½ miles.

CHAPTER 3

the next lecture. I got to The Crescent for tea and spent the evening as stated.

Wednesday September 11th (50th day).

Wrote to Mr. Hill who was a fellow-passenger of mine on the *Ormuz*. He is leaving by steamer for Melbourne on Saturday, and I am asking him to stay another fortnight and go back with me on the *Ortona*, also wrote to my wife's uncle – Mr. T. Hind – and to Mr. Willis saying how deeply I regret not being able to visit Darlington again. Got my slides arranged during the morning, and in the afternoon I went to Ponteland where I had tea with Mr. and Mrs. Jameson, where we sat chatting till bedtime.

Thursday September 12th (51st day).

Wrote to the Hon. J. G. Ward, minister for Railways, and to my dear wife, and at 7.30 again lectured at Ponteland in the Anglican School Room, the Rev. F. W. Langton again taking the chair. The subjects dealt with, were: The Land question, Lumber Industry, Mineral Wealth, Sheep Farming and the Timber Industry, and Recent Legislation. There was again a good attendance, though not quite so large as on Monday last.

After the lecture I called on Mrs. Forester[90], who before her marriage, was considered to be the belle of the village, and afterwards called on my uncle, now 73 years of age, and is as cheerful and healthy as when I left England in 1873. He

---

[90] Bessie Moorhead.

has read a good deal for one in his position, has a good memory and a fair portion of shrewd native common sense. He and his housekeeper have been uncommonly kind, and the visits I have paid them have given me more than ordinary pleasure.

Friday September 13th (52nd day).

Walked out to Dissington Tile Sheds this morning where I again saw Mr. and Mrs. Bowling, and bid them good bye, then returned to Ponteland and had lunch with Mr. and Mrs. Jameson, then called on a few of the old villagers and bid them good bye, and shortly after my dear brother Jack and I set off for Newcastle, he pushing his bike the whole distance rather than I should walk alone. At Wolsingham bridge, we smoked our pipes while we rested, and this delightful half hour will remain a bright spot in my memory while life shall last.

We arrived at Newcastle at 8 p.m., my brother going through to Washington, and I to The Crescent.

Saturday September 14 (53rd day).

Spent the forenoon at The Crescent, and at 1.30 met my brother at the Railway offices in Neville St., and then we drove to Washington, by way of Sheriff, Wreckenton, Eighton Banks, Springwell and Ulsworth. The drive was delightful, for I had lived in the district when a young man. St. John's Church at Sheriff Hill is a conspicuous object, and on a clear day, I am told, it can be seen from many parts of Northumberland, Durham and Gosforth. The first debating

CHAPTER 3

society of which I was a member met at Wreckenton. The first sermon I preached with the object of becoming a local preacher, was at Ulsworth. I state these facts to show how interesting the drive would be. We got to Washington at 6 p.m.

The following particulars were given me today by Mrs. J. W. Laws: John William Laws born at Ponteland February 1st 1852; Mary Dickenson, wife of the above, born at Cox Green, June 15th 1857, the above were married at the Registry Office Gateshead; Robert Montgomery born September 2nd 1879, Assistant Rate Collector, Gateshead; Coningsby born May 2nd 1881, Commercial Traveller; Helen born Jan 14th 1883, Coxon Bo's Mantle Rooms; Norman born February 1st 1885, Clerk in water rate office, Gateshead. The above are my brother's children by a former marriage.[91]

President McKinley died today.[92]

Sunday September 15th (54th day).

No Record

Monday September 16th (55th day).

We are now in the middle of September, and the time of my departure draweth nigh, and I will be glad to get back to my loved ones in New Zealand, yet sorry to leave the many friends and relatives I have met in this country.

---

[91] His former wife was Barbara Shanks Richardson (1851–1887).

[92] He died from gangrene resulting from the gunshot wounds.

Spent most of the forenoon in arranging slides and in otherwise preparing for my lantern lecture at Biddick tomorrow.

In the afternoon Mr. Dickinson and I went to see a new shaft that is being sunk for a new colliery that is expected to start soon, but in sinking this shaft the workmen have encountered a quicksand of several feet. This could not be cut through in the ordinary way, and the difficulty can only be got over by freezing it into a solid mass and then cutting it through. A German firm has undertaken to do this by a new process in which ammonia is the chief factor. I fear the sketch (Figure 48, see also Figure 49) will give more mirth than information, but having no compass pen I had to resort to a primitive method.

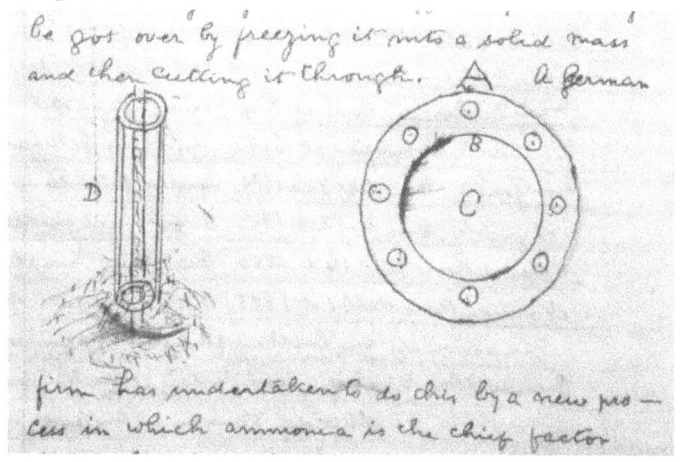

Figure 48 The German device for freezing quicksand. (Laws Family Collection).

The outer ring A is supposed to represent the crib work, the inside of the shaft is 24 feet in diameter. The small

CHAPTER 3

circles, show the freezing pipes, one of which I have tried to enlarge at D, the circle C, which is 12 feet in diameter, shows the size of the shaft when complete. To carry out the work the contractors had to provide several cylinders in each of which was a coil of pipe 675 feet long, made in one piece. The freezing process is very plainly seen at cylinder at D.

I lectured in Wesleyan Sunday School. at Biddick to a large audience at 8 p.m. The subject being "Lecture No 1. The Discovery of New Zealand, Colonization, The Maories." The chair was taken by J. Lowd Esq. Jack and his son Norman had charge of the lantern and everything passed off satisfactorily.

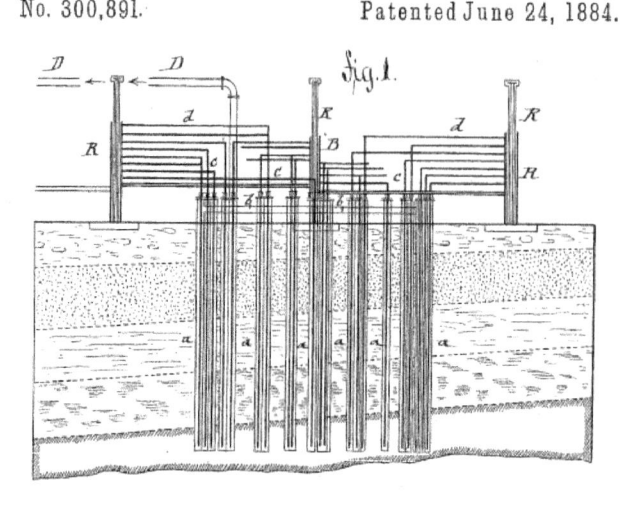

Figure 49 The German device for freezing quicksand from U.S. patent number 300891 of 1884. (United States patent office).

Tuesday September 17th (56th day).

Last evening I lectured in the Wesley Hall at Biddick. I dealt chiefly with the Maori race, the subject being the discovery and colonization of New Zealand, and there was a large audience. After returning to Washington although the hour was late, I put a number of slides through at the request of my brother, this was done in order that Mr. and Mrs. Dickinson might have a look at them and have some idea of what had been going on at the lectures for they, being now stricken in years and not able to be present, would be pleased to see the nature of the entertainment.

Wednesday September 18th (57th day).

I cleaned my lantern and slides this morning, and in the afternoon we had quite a large family party. The first to arrive were my sisters Sallie, Susannah and Lil, and not long after, my brother Jack and Coulthard made their appearances and then followed in quick succession my nephews, Monty, Con and Norman, and niece Helen. Then came Mr. and Mrs. Dickinson[93] with their granddaughters, Gertie, Nellie and May. My dear sister brought letters from the following friends and relatives, Eva, Mabel, Bertha, H. Mole, E. Banks, James Stobert, Edward Walker and Miss. Robinson, also a photo of Munroe Street sent by Mr. James Davis of Greenmeadows.

---

[93] These are relatives of Jack's second wife, with whom he had no children.

CHAPTER 3

Thursday September 19th (58th day).

Jack and I drove to Ulsworth Station this morning and then by train to Newcastle, where I spent most of the day at The Crescent, and George played several of his compositions, and songs that he had set to music. George and Bert seem to occupy prominent positions in the musical circles of the north.

In the afternoon I wrote to Mr. Cunnold, Tenterden; Messrs. Clarke Burnham, re Beecroft's pamphlet; T. Renayne Esq., General Manager New Zealand Railways; Hon. Sir Joseph Ward, Minister for Railways. Mr. Thorpe, re lantern lecture at the People's Hall, "Rye Hill", and a Post Card to Jack re photo group.

Friday September 20th (59th day).

I called on the following friends this morning:— Mr. W. Plews, Mr. Harras a late employer of mine, Nellie Fletcher, Mrs. Womack – a sister of the Rev. John Reay – and in the afternoon my sister and I went to Heaton and saw Mrs. A. E. Common, widow of the late Mr. A. E. Common[94] of Kenton Bank Foot.

After tea we walked to the Hay Market and then by cab to The Crescent. I report not to have seen Heaton Park, which is said to be the loveliest in Newcastle. Heaton Park was presented to the town by the late Sir William Armstrong, a large portion of it had formerly formed part of the famous Jesmond Dene. When we got home we found half a dozen

---

[94] With whom Thomas served his apprenticeship.

copies of "The Daily Leader" containing a report of the interview at my brother's office on September 6th.

Saturday September 21st (60th day).

Met my brother in town and after a cup of tea we set off to walk to Ponteland, and when in Newgate Street I missed my companion, and after waiting a few minutes I saw him hurrying toward me with a face as radiant as a north west moon. He had slipped into a tobacconist shop and bought me a pipe, the counterpart of his own, which I had to use at once and we went on our way puffing the fragrant weed. It rained a little, which to some extent marred our enjoyment, but the companionship was delightful and the road was interestingly familiar.

About 5 p.m. we got to the Bank Foot where as usual we were hospitably entertained by Mrs. Jameson. Rain was now falling heavily, but we pushed on until we were fortunately overtaken by Mr. Smith of Milburn who very kindly took us into his trap to the end of our journey. We got to the village about 6.30, and spent some time with my uncle Willie, John and Martin Jameson, and finally arrived at the house of Mr. James Stobert, whose guests we are to be until we leave for Newcastle on Monday.

Sunday September 22nd (61st day).

Jack and I went to the Sunday School at 9 a.m., when my brother gave an address, and after school Mr. Stobert accompanied my brother and me to the village church, where the Rev. F. W. Langton preached a nice little sermon. In the

Chapter 3

evening I took the service at the Methodist Church, and had a fair amount of liberty, my brother taking the opening exercises. I was delighted, and no doubt he was the same, that we should stand together in the pulpit amid scenes and memories so inspiring.

I was also delighted to meet Mr. Stobert, who from my childhood, had been my spiritual guide, philosopher and friend, and who for more than 30 years had been Society Steward, Sunday School Superintendent, and precentor. In addition to what I have stated, we went to the class-meeting in the afternoon where we had a happy and profitable time.

We sleep tonight at Mr. Stobert's and leave for Newcastle in the morning, so this is probably the last night in the "Mecca" of my earthly hope.

Monday September 23rd (62nd day).

After breakfast my brother and I left Ponteland intending to walk to Newcastle, but on reaching the Bank Foot Mr. Jameson very kindly took us to town in his trap, and the rest of the morning I spent at The Crescent in arranging my slides for my lecture tonight.

In the afternoon I met Jack, Sallie and Susan, with their respective families, at Hewitt's Photographic Studio, where we sat for a large family group (Figure 50). Besides those already mentioned there were present. Mr. and Mrs. J. W. Laws, Mr. M. Laws, Mr. Con Laws, Miss. Helen Laws, Mr. and Mrs. Coulthard, Mrs. Farmiloe jun., Messrs. George and Bert Dodds, Mr. Joseph Farmiloe (son of the above).

This group will probably be regarded as an heirloom in the family. It was taken at my brother's suggestion.

Unfortunately the family of my youngest sister[95] is unrepresented on account of sickness, and there are a few others who could not get away on account of business claims.

---

[95] Elizabeth Jane Thompson née Laws.

CHAPTER 3

Figure 50 The 1901 family photograph. In the front row
Thomas Laws is third from the left and Jack is fifth. More
details are given in Appendix 3. (Robert Laws Collection).

I got the 5 p.m. to Washington, where I lectured on the Hot Lake District, or Wonderland of New Zealand. The chair was taken by Joseph Gibson Esq. of Manchester. My brother Jack was in charge of the lantern. There was a good attendance, and the entertainment gave general satisfaction.

Tuesday September 24th (63rd day).

Arranged my slides for my lecture at Ponteland on 30th *inst.* and then came to Newcastle. At the Central Station I met Mr. Gibson, my chairman of yesterday, and we took the train to Whitley hoping to spend a little time with Mr. John Newlands, but unfortunately he had gone to Leeds on business, however Mrs. Newlands gave us a hearty welcome, and attended to our requirements. Mr. Newlands junior has just been transferred to the Post Office at Leeds to a similar position as he recently held in the Post Office at Whitley.

Miss. Newlands is shortly to be married. Miss. Agnes the youngest of the family attended to our wants, and we had a few happy hours together. Mrs. Newlands gave me a family photo to remind me of my Whitley friends. We arrived at Newcastle at 8.30 p.m., then went to The Crescent, there being no train to Washington at that hour.

Wednesday September 25th (64th day).

Wrote to the Rev. F. W. Langton and Mr. John Dees, also to Mr. T. H. Bainbridge, and after lunch went to the Manors Station, and called on Mr. and Mrs. Gibson who is the mother of Mr. M. Spriggs of Napier, we talked a little about New Zealand and a good deal about her boy in Napier.

Chapter 3

I then went to the Shipping Office and booked my passage to Tilbury, and will leave Newcastle October 7th by the RMS *Ortona*.

I have been strongly tempted to stay another fortnight, but all things considered it will be best to leave as above so as to get back to New Zealand not later than November 30th. Had tea at Dunstan where we had another family gathering when the following were present: Jack and Mary, my sister, Mrs. Dodds, Mr. and Mrs. Coulthard, Mr. and Mrs. Farmiloe, Mr. and Mrs. Thompson, Monty and Helen, Joe Farmiloe, Flossie Bolland[96].

These family gatherings are delightful, and will revive pleasant memories, while life lasts. I stayed all night at Coulthards.

Thursday September 26th (65th day).

Mrs. Coulthard and I went to Bentinck Crescent where we stayed for lunch, and then to the central Station, where we expected to meet Mr. J. Smith, a fellow passenger with me in the *Ormuz*, but he failed to appear. We then returned to Dunstan, where Mr. Farmiloe showed us all over the large mill of which he is manager. We then returned to Mr. Coulthard's residence at Dunstan, where we had a pleasant musical evening.

---

[96] Daughter of Elizabeth Jane by her first husband.

Friday September 27th (66th day).

Came in from Dunstan this morning, and went to the Tyne General Shipping Office to see Mr. Stephenson on behalf of his brother in New Zealand, but Mr. Stephenson being out of town I was not able to see him. I am acquainted with his brother, formerly of Napier NZ, now of New Plymouth, from whom I had a letter of introduction.

I next went to Market Street, where I had arranged to meet Mr Tom Bainbridge at his place of business, but met with a second disappointment for, like Mr Stephenson, Mr Bainbridge was also out of town. I then returned to Dunstan where I had intended to spend the day, but I got a wire from Mrs. Dodds saying that Mr. and Mrs. J. B. Bowes were expecting my sister and me to spend the evening, so my sister and I went over and had a very pleasant evening.

Mr. Bowes has been choir master at Blenheim Street Wesleyan Chapel for the last forty years and still retains that position. My wife has known him from her childhood. Our conversation was principally about old times, and the chapel friends we knew between 30 and 40 years ago.

Saturday September 28th (67th day).

Met my brother Jack in town, and we went to Watson's in Grainger Street, and got the carbide[97] that was required for my next lecture. At 12.45 we had lunch with Mr. T. H. Bainbridge at his place of business in Market St., and then

---

[97] Calcium carbide, for the acetylene lamp of the magic lantern.

Chapter 3

we met Mr. Wm Jameson, who took us in his trap to Ponteland. Had supper with Mr. and Mrs. Forester.

When I was a lad living in the village, I was well acquainted with the present Mrs. Forester, who was then "Bessie Moorhead" and by general consent was regarded as the belle of the village. She and I were then members of a quadrille party that met every Saturday night in the long room of the Seven Stars Inn for practice. We were also members of the Church of England choir, in which Miss Moorhead was one of the sopranos and I played the clarinet.

There was then no organ in the church, but this lack was supplied in a measure by several instrumentalists who at the conclusion of the band practice, remained for an hour to practice hymns, anthems, and general music for the following Sunday, and among those who gave this voluntary assistance I remember the following:

> James Daud, *schoolmaster*, first violin; William Charlton, *shoemaker*, 1st violin; John Jameson, *parish clerk* (and uncle of John×, Martin, and William Jameson so frequently mentioned in this diary), 1st clarinet; Thos Reay, *village blacksmith*, 1st violin, (uncle of the Rev John Reay); John Jameson (my chum), 1st violin (just mentioned and marked by the cross×); Martin Jameson, brother of the above; Russell Warburton, *saddler*, bass viol; Joseph Henderson, *village carpenter*, piccolo; William Laidman, *stone mason*, 2nd clarinet (and flute); Cornelius Bowring, flute; Robert Laws, clarinet; Thomas Laws[98], son of the above, 1st clarinet;

---

[98] The author of these diaries.

> Thomas Laws, Smallburn, 1st violin, No relation to the preceding Thomas Laws.

These were the noble men, who for some years represented the organ in the parish church without receiving fee or thanks. After leaving the Forester's, I had an hour's chat with my dear old friend and playmate, John Jameson, whose life seems to be fast ebbing out and it distresses me to think that possibly this may be the last time that I shall look upon his face, or take him by the hand.

Then I went up the village to the house of his brother, Martin, whose guest I am to be while at Ponteland. It distresses me to think that probably this is the last visit I will make to what is for me the dearest spot on this earth.

Sunday September 29th (68th day).

Mr. Martin Jameson and I walked as far as the Dissington Tile Sheds, and spent an hour with Mr. and Mrs. Bowing, and then returned to the village, and in the afternoon we went to the village Chapel, where Mr. T. Richardson preached from Heb IV, 9. "There remaineth therefore a rest for the people of God." After tea, Mr Jameson and I drove to Milburn for the following reasons:

1st My father was born not only in the village, but most likely in the very building now used as a chapel.

2nd My uncle Tom died at Milburn[99] on Oct 26th 1840. I have heard my mother say that my Christian name was to

---

[99] Milbourne and Milburn appear to be the same place. Both spellings are used by Thomas.

Chapter 3

have been "John", but my uncle dying before I was baptized, I was named after him.

3rd My grandfather and grandmother lived for many years in this building, and their family of four sons and three daughters were born in it.

4th The first sermon I remember to have heard, was preached here, from the words "The effectual fervent prayer of a righteous man, availeth much." At this time my father farmed Kirkley West Farm, and I would be about seven or eight years of age, and the distance to Milbourne being only about a couple of miles we walked over together there this Sunday morning.

5th My first attempt to preach was here, on May 26th 1861. My text being Rom XII.I "I beseech you therefore brethren by the mercy of God, that ye present yourselves a living sacrifice, holy and acceptable unto God which is your reasonable service." It is also worthy of remark, that the same dear friend who accompanied me that day, 40 years ago took me in his trap today, and I have not been in the chapel from that day to this.[100]

After service we had a cup of tea at Mr. Smith's, Mr. Jameson going to Ponteland and I to Kirkley Cottages,

---

[100] In another copy of his 1901 diary, Thomas gives the following information, which has been corrected in some details by Derek Laws: My father, born at Milburn December 4th, 1815, died Dunstan Gateshead in 1885; Sarah wife of the above died June 21st, 1891. Susannah (2nd), their daughter, died at Ponteland September 25th, 1903. Elizabeth Jane, daughter of the above died Sept 21st, 1911; Isabella Laws, wife of brother Robert died at Napier August 11th, 1931.

where I hope to spend tomorrow with my cousin Tom, his wife, and their daughter Mollie.

Monday September 30th (69th day).

Spent most of the day with my cousin and his family at Kirkley Cottages, and at 4 p.m. walked to Ponteland only about two and half miles distant. My cousin is a market gardener and disposes of his products at the Newcastle market, his principal line being strawberries and maidenhair fern. I was pleased to look through his garden and greenhouses and brought away a maidenhair fern, and a few prize peas that I hope to grow in New Zealand.

I called on Miss. Brown, who is the daughter of my last schoolmaster, Mr. Ralph Brown, and had the pleasure looking at a photo of his well-remembered features, and again the beautiful specimens of his handwriting. I then went to centre of the village and had tea with my dear old uncle and his housekeeper, and lecture in the Methodist Chapel on "The Wonderland of New Zealand."

Mr. Smith and family came down from Milbourne, Mr. John Fletcher had walked from Breckney Hill, Jon Wheatman from Prestwick, Mr. W. Jameson and family from Kenton and Catterick, my brother Jack and his son Con cycled from Newcastle, Tom Wheatman from Prestwick.

Before the lecture, Jack and I had a walk up Callerton Lane, and what was said and felt cannot be set down in cold pen and ink. Dear old Jack, I will never forget this walk, neither will I forget the kindness you have shown me during the last ten weeks. God bless you old boy, and every member

Chapter 3

of your family, and lifting up the light of His countenance upon you will be the prayer of your brother Tom until we bid each other good morning where "farewell words are never spoken, where parted hands are clasped again."

Tuesday October 1st (70th day).

Before leaving Ponteland I thought I would like to take one fond last lingering look at my beloved Mecca, and on that sacred spot I inwardly quoted David's lament over Jerusalem (Psalms 13 verses 5 and 6) and I deeply sympathize with him in his grief.

In my village walk I began by walking round the field known as the "The Croft", a field at the west end of the village, in which "Ponteland Races" were sometimes held, a horse named "Lady Leticia", owned by my Uncle Willie, I remembered running on one occasion, but she was not placed. I then crossed the turnpike and went down Pont Lonnen, as far as the river, where the lane or "lonnen" terminates, it being only about 50 or 60 yards long and leading to foot bridge giving access to Fenwick Fatkin's market gardens. I did not cross the river (Pont). I then went down Allen's Close as far as "The Steps", or steeping stones, laid in a shallow part of the river for the convenience of persons who had allotments on the opposite side of the river, in a piece of ground named "Van Diemen's Land."

VISITING ENGLAND IN 1901

Figure 51 The Methodist Chapel in Ponteland. The river is in flood. (Photographer: unknown, Ponteland Local History Society Archives, reproduced with permission).

I then returned to Jameson's where I found that Mr. Bowing had sent his trap to be at our disposal for the day of perfect enjoyment. First we went down the village as far as Clickemin Bridge, then up the north lane, past the Church, in which I was baptized, and Eland Green, where I was born. On we went and past in succession, The Buildings, Smallburn, Michael's Shop, The Foot Hill, Kirkley West farm[101], Highham Dykes, The Highlander, where we sat in the shade ate our lunch, then on to Milbourne Grange, Milbourne village.

My dear old uncle proved to be a most interesting travelling companion, and being intimate with every detail of the road, was able to give us a good deal of local information. We went down Milbourne Lane, and we

---

[101] That is World's End farm.

Chapter 3

reached the turnpike leading to Ponteland, where we arrived about 4.30, and then my uncle packed up a lot of bulbs and chrysanthemums for me to take to New Zealand.

Mr. Martin Jameson then took me in the same conveyance, to the Mill Farm, on Prestwick Carr, where I bid Mrs. Stewart (formerly Bella Dodds) good bye, and we got back to the village at 8.30 p.m. Then I crossed the street and said good bye to the Temperleys and the Mackeys, had just a few minutes with my dear old friend John Jameson, who is so unwell that I fear his end is drawing nigh, he had gone to bed. He had left me several photos that I was pleased to get for they keep in memory several of my old friends, and especially of Mr. Jameson himself. I got to my hosts' about 10.30 where I expect to sleep for the last time in England.

Wednesday October 2nd (71st day).

Leaving Ponteland: Bid good bye to Mr. Stobert and my uncle Willie, John and Martin Jameson, their wives and families, also to Annie Boiston and Tom Robson. John Jameson was unable to come down, so I went to his room and had a few parting words with him. Before I got away Mrs. Martin Jameson filled a small bottle with Pont water that I may take it to New Zealand, as a reminder of my long connection with the village. According to previous arrangement, my cousin Tom arrived from Kirkley cottages at 9 a.m., and we left the dear old spot so plentifully strewed with hallowed memories.

All with whom I came into contact have vied with each other to make my visit a time of special enjoyment. I got my last look at the village from what is known locally as The Round Hill gate, and as we went down the hill on the Newcastle side, the rising ground behind us shut out the view to be seen no more by me for ever.

I got to The Crescent by 11 a.m., and went to Dunstan in the afternoon, where I spent the rest of the day until 10 p.m., when I got the ferry-boat and crossed the river and reached The Crescent about 10.30.

Thursday October 3rd (72nd day).

I am reminded by the date that this my 61st Birthday. I spent most of the day in packing up and putting my lantern slides in order for the lecture at the People's Hall, and afterwards went to the Hall and completed the arrangements, and at the appointed time I lectured to the largest company I have yet had. Here I met Willie Chapman, Jim Spence, and Willie Plews and several others, who were making enquiries about New Zealand.

During the afternoon I bought three watches, one each for my wife, Mabel, and Bertha, and also a few necessary things for use during the voyage. On getting to The Crescent, I found that my sister had also had been making a few purchases, namely a copy each of Tennyson and Whittier, which she very kindly asked me to accept as a token of her affection.

Friday October 4th (73rd day).

Met Arnold Bowes at what was formerly Blenheim Street Wesleyan Chapel, but has since been purchased by the

Chapter 3

Education Department, and is now being used as a public school. This building has a special interest for me; I attended its services from 1863 to 1870, and sometimes took the pulpit. My dear wife, then Miss. M. A. Newlands had attended the Sunday School, and the public services from her earliest recollection, and it was here I first made her acquaintance, and here our eldest son was baptized by the Rev. Thomas Vasey, and as I mentally surveyed the building, I filled the seats with their occupants in those distant days.

At the suggestion of Mr. Bowes I was photographed in the pew that my wife and I had been accustomed to occupy, and had she been included, my cup of happiness would have overflowed. The chapel was sold to the Education Board several years ago, and the congregation either bought or built the People's Hall, where they now worship. After being photographed by Mr. Bowes, I sent my luggage to the Forth Railway from which it will dispatched to Tilbury.

In the evening my sister and I called on Mr. and Mrs. Edward Brown and bad them goodbye. Mr. Brown is the son of the school teacher and we talked about our former games "and fought our battles over again", until it was time to meet Mr. T. Spence, with whom I had an appointment. Mr. Spence was one of the scholars in my senior class, and we had a very interesting chat about former times. He is now a local preacher, but what pleased me above all, was to hear from his own lips that I was the means of leading him to the Saviour.

Saturday October 5th (74th day).

Spent most of the day with my sister at The Crescent, and left about 4 p.m. for the house of Mr. and Mrs. Thompson. The latter is my youngest sister, and in addition to our host and hostess, there were present: Edie and Florence Bollard, my brother Jack and his sons, Monty, Con and Norman and his daughter Helen, Mrs. Dodds and her son Bert, and a friend whose name did not transfer, also a number of young people who are connected with The Primitive Methodist Church, Mr. and Mrs. Councillor Carr. I am humbled when I think of the honour that is being bestowed upon so unworthy a guest. After spending a very pleasant evening, my sister and I walked to Newcastle where we arrived at 10.30 p.m.

Sunday October 6th (75th day).

As I leave for London tomorrow, I may fairly say this is my last day in the north of England. At 10.30 I preached at Dunstan, where my dear brother Jack took the opening and closing exercises, the family being well represented. There were present Sallie, George and Bert Dodds, my brother Jack and his wife, Mr. and Mrs. Coulthard, my sister Lizzy and her husband. During the afternoon the young people began to arrive, among whom were Helen, Monty, Con, Norman, Flossie, Edie Bollard, Joe Coulthard and his young lady – Jennie, Nellie Fletcher, Ella Willson, Mollie Laws from Kirkley cottage and a few others who names I did not obtain. Nearly all present could sing and play, and during the afternoon, with George and Bert at the piano, we had some

CHAPTER 3

capital singing. My sister Sallie had a splendid voice in her younger days, and when the United Choirs of Northumberland and Durham gave their annual concert in Town Hall, Newcastle, she frequently took the part of leading soprano. Fred and Mrs. Farmiloe, could sing and also play well, and the singing of Miss. Ella Willson was simply a revelation, and surpassed anything of the kind I had ever heard. Miss. Willson is the leading soprano in my nephew's choir at Elswick Road all the young people went to their respective churches, and the rest of us did not have a happy time, in view of our early separation.

We met again at supper and not long afterwards our leave-taking began. But over this I must draw a veil except to say that it was the least desirable part of the day's proceedings. I suppose I felt the parting words especially hard to say, for all present were very dear to me and their kindness will be fragrant memory if and when I am permitted to reach my distant home in New Zealand.

Monday October 7th (76th day).

I have had many red letter days during the time I have been in England, but around this I feel like putting a broad black border. I have anticipated this day for some time and especially during the last few weeks, but failed to realize its full significance, and I never expected our parting would be so sad and depressing. The last forty-eight hours has almost made me regret that I ever left Tyneside.[102]

---

[102] Presumably he is referring to 1873.

VISITING ENGLAND IN 1901

Immediately after breakfast, I got a postal order cashed that had come from Mr. Clarke Burnham of Morpeth. I then bought a pair of leather straps, gathered all my loose luggage, bid my dear sister a last affectionate adieu, and at 9.40, accompanied by George and Bert Dodds, began my homeward journey. On arrival at the Central Station, I found my dear brother Jack and his two sons waiting to bid me God speed, and the last of the many kind gifts I received was a pencil-case from George, and tobacco pouch from Con.

I left by the 10.5 express, and as we waved our handkerchiefs to each other as we crossed High Leven[103] and lost sight of each other, the blackness of midnight settled upon my soul. The last 48 hours has almost made me wish I had never left New Zealand[104], the agony of parting being almost too big a price to pay for the all too brief enjoyment of the old scenes and friends of former times.

The first station at which we stopped was Durham, then Darlington, Northallerton, York, Selby, Doncaster, Peterborough, Finsbury Park, and lastly at Kings Cross, where we arrived at about 5 p.m. There I found my old Napier friend Mrs. E. Walker, waiting and we took to her residence, 77 Constantine Road. This family, consisting of Mr. and Mrs. Walker and their two sons, George and William, were our shipmates on they *Douglas* to New Zealand in 1873, and like ourselves settled in Napier. He was a

---

[103] High Leven Bridge, a two tier structure designed by Robert Stephenson.

[104] That is to say, he almost regrets revisiting Tyneside because it is so painful to leave again.

Chapter 3

Wesleyan Sunday School teacher and also a Trustee, and being members of the same church and congregation we were intimately acquainted.

Figure 52 Heading south by train in the winter. (Photographer: Dr. Tice F. Budden 1889–1923, The Budden Collection, National Railway Museum, supplied by John Alsop).

I am comforting myself tonight with the hope of soon being with my loved ones in the land of my adoption and with the richer hope at last all gathering in that land "where farewell words are never spoken; where parted hands are clasped again."

Tuesday October 8th (77th day).

Mrs. Walker went with me to Charing Cross, where I left my trunk and parcel, and then to Trafalgar Square, where we had a look at the lions on Nelson's monument. Then a hurried run through the National Gallery, and continued our ramble by way of The Horse Guards, where we witnessed the ceremony of Changing Guard. Then to The Houses of

Parliament, where at 11.30 we were looking at Big Ben, and lastly to Westminster, where "Forty generations lie sleeping." The walls are covered with tablets in memory of the illustrious dead:- Palmerston, James Fox, William Pitt, Sir Isaac Newton, Major Andre, John Wesley, Charles Wesley, etc., etc., etc., but I forgot to look for the "Lia Fail" or Stone of Destiny, and before leaving the Abbey, we saw the Royal Tombs. Then along the Thames Embankment as far as Cleopatra's Needle and Westminster Bridge, and returned to Constantine road at 4.30 p.m.

Wednesday October 9th (78th day).

After breakfast, with Mrs. John Walker as guide went to St. Paul's Cathedral, had a look at London Bridge, saw the London monument, The Bank of England, City Road Chapel, The Wesleyan Book depot. Then to Cannon Street, where I booked for Tenterden by the Rother Valley at 12.48. Part of the journey, was on the London and South Coast Railway, as far as Robertsbridge, then to Tenterden by the Rother Valley.

We arrived at our destination about 4 p.m. I walked from the station to the town, and on the way I met Mr. Cunnold, who was on the look-out for me, and after a cup of tea a hearty welcome from Mrs. Cunnold, he and I had a look at the town, which is a quaint old fashioned place, but beautiful for situation and scrupulously clean, and while we stood looking at old church the chimes sweetly played "The Last Rose of Summer", and after our return to Mr. Cunnold's home, we spent a very agreeable evening.

CHAPTER 3

Figure 53 The Bank of England (left) and the Royal Exchange (right) *circa* **1900. (Keystone View Company, Robert Laws Collection).**

My host is also father of my son in law who is agent for the Beale sewing machine in Hastings, a position he has held for several years. My host was pleased to hear all I could tell him about New Zealand, and I was pleased to tell them what I knew about Mr. and Mrs. Cunnold who are so well and favourably known in Hastings, New Zealand.

Thursday October 10th (79th day).

Mr. Cunnold and I had a long, leisurely, stroll in Tenterden today, and also spent some time in the Park. I like the quaint old town, and the Park is well kept, but in my opinion I would give Darlington the pre-eminence.

VISITING ENGLAND IN 1901

Mr. Cunnold gave me a cutting of a very pretty plant, that I hope to get safely to New Zealand.

After a cup of tea with my genial host and hostess, and me having bid the latter good bye, Mr. Cunnold accompanied me to the Railway Station. I had time only to bid him a hurried farewell. Our train started for Charing Cross at 5.25 and got to its destination at 8.50. I then took tram to the Mansfield Hotel and walked the short distance to Coronation Road, packed my portmanteaus, had supper, a long farewell talk, joined in family prayer, and then off to bed at midnight.

At Tenterden there are some of the most curious, old fashioned houses I have ever seen. The roofs appear to be all broken-backed in a fashion that I cannot describe, and are covered with old, flat tiles. Whether they are watertight or not I cannot say but am very doubtful. Sent a post card from Tenterden to my sister, Mrs. Dodds.

Left Constantine road at 8.15 a.m., and accompanied by Mrs. John Walker, got to Railway Station at St. Pancras at 8:45 and got all my luggage safely on the train, but it was not until 11:15 that we arrived at Tilbury.

4. Returning to New Zealand in 1901

Figure 54 Daily positions of the SS *Ortona* and SS *Talune* on the voyage from England to New Zealand in 1901. (Courtesy Darrin Ward and Google).

Friday October 11th, 1901 (1st day on my return journey).

At Tilbury I was pleased to meet Joseph Gilbertson, and John Penrose, also Joseph Emerson, who were fellow passenger with me in the *Ormuz*. We were all speedily aboard, and at 12.30 (midday) we started on our Homeward voyage.

CHAPTER 4

The usual parting scenes were witnessed on the wharf: crowds of people waving their handkerchiefs and following the vessel to the furthest possible limit of safety, some laughing and jesting, as though the scene was comic opera, while others seemed inexpressibly sad, and tears were swimming down the cheeks of not a few.

The weather was cold and threatening, but the sea was peaceful, and we steamed down the Channel, as smoothly, as a "painted ship upon a painted ocean", but with a speed that bore testimony to the rapidity with which certain well remembered land-marks were left behind. So far I am favourably impressed with the *Ortona*, her passengers and crew. Got two letters, one each from Mr. Brydene and Miss. Minton; these were delivered on board.

Figure 55 The RMS *Ortona* in 1907. Thomas sailed on her from London to Sydney. (Photographer: unknown, John Oxley Library, State Library of Queensland, item 1-157625, from Wikipedia).

Returning to New Zealand in 1901

Saturday October 12th (2nd day).

After a pleasant run down the Channel, we arrived at Plymouth at 11 a.m. Here we took on board a number of passengers and a good deal of general cargo, and at about 5.30 p.m. we bid adieu to the English coast, and the last we saw of England was the Eddystone lighthouse which was visible for a good while after losing sight of the English Coast. The last to come on board, were Mr. James Brown and another whose name I did not obtain, they were fellow passengers in the *Ormuz*.

Sunday October 13th (3rd day).

Weather cold and ship rolling badly and many suffering from sea sickness, but so far I have escaped that experience, my present trouble being that I cannot locate my warm clothing. This was packed in a trunk and sent on board labelled "cabin" and now cannot be found, but the steward assures me it is on board and no doubt with turn up all right.

The *Ortona* is in every respect a much better boat than the *Ormuz*. She is a new boat and therefore cleaner, she is also larger, and both accommodation and food are superior to the *Ormuz*. The crew are more civil, and the passengers more agreeable. We have run since leaving Plymouth 242 miles.

Monday October 14th (4th day).

Weather cold and wet, but the sea is quiet and we are settling down to the routine of a long voyage. I am told there are 1100 souls on board: 800 passengers and a crew of 300.

Chapter 4

My lost trunk turned up today, I had also lost a small pocket book given me by my brother, but it also has come to hand. Our run today is 307 miles.

Tuesday October 15th (5th day).

Weather is fine though breezy. We have been going along the coast of Portugal all day, and just got a glance at Lisbon as we passed, and a little further south, there were large, scattered buildings, said to be a monastery. We were passing Cape St. Vincent at 3 p.m. During the afternoon, a dove and four starlings alighted on the rigging, the poor things were not molested, for which I was surprised and thankful. Several steamers and sailing vessels were sighted, and also a large French battleship, which we saluted by dipping our ensign as a courtesy to the Frenchman who responded readily.

One of the passengers is from Washington County Durham and says he knows my brother Jack and he is taking a voyage to Australia for the good of his health. I find there are two passengers on board who sailed with us on the *Ormuz*: One is a First Class passenger and the other a quartermaster I have chummed with, a nice young fellow named Bate, he is a Wesleyan, married, and hails from Melbourne.

At noon we were 229 miles distant from Gibraltar our position then being 37° 30' N, 9° 19' W. Run for the last 24 hours 284 miles.

Wednesday October 16th (6th day).

We arrived at Gibraltar at daylight, and from our present position the Rock is seen from a slightly different point of view than on the occasion previously given.

At noon today we were 24 miles from Gibraltar 36° 10' N, 4° 45' W. Run 24 miles.

Saw several swallows when coming through the straits, these probably being the pioneers of the southern migration that begins about this time toward the warmer latitudes of the South. Wrote to my sister, Mrs. Coulthard, and hope to post at Marseilles tomorrow.

Thursday October 17th (7th day).

Weather fine and a stiff breeze blowing. After dinner I went on deck, and got a good view of the Balearic Islands, which we were passing from 11 a.m. until 2 p.m., and an hour later, a waterspout was seen about three miles ahead.

At first what we saw was an inky looking black cloud, dropped from a larger black cloud from above. The sea below now became violently agitated and drawn up as though it were a hill of water that every minute was increasing in size, and the sea for a considerable distance from the centre of the disturbance became more and more agitated, the column from below rising and that from above continuing to come down until the two columns met. After that I have no idea what occurred, except that the column continued to be unbroken for about fifteen or twenty minutes when it parted about midway, the upper half being drawn into the cloud and the lower descending into the sea.

CHAPTER 4

Posted letter to my sisters Mrs. Coulson and Mrs. Thompson. I now find that letters may be posted on the high seas, and only require a penny stamp.

Figure 56 A group of waterspouts. (Engraver: James Pollard Espy, The Philosophy of Storms 1841, from Wikipedia).

Friday October 18th (8th day).

Arrived at Marseilles about 11.30. The weather is beautiful and we saw the city to better advantage than on July 16. The trees are still beautiful in their foliage, which does not appear to be chilled by the breath of autumn. We saw the same churches and public buildings "la Virge de la Garde" is an imposing structure, with its wide circular headed gateway surmounted by massive towers and its elegant dome being objects that at once attract attention, and surmounting the dome is the large statue of the "Virgin on Guard" as though keeping watch over the city and harbour. Fort Larrima[105] lay at little farther to the east and from the fort there rises a circular lighthouse.

It seems a pity that on these large ocean liners no information is given concerning objects of interest to be seen on the voyage. How much more interesting would such travelling be if, each day, the passengers knew the name of any island, town when in port, or lighthouse we were likely to pass, and the name and purpose of the principal buildings. I have no doubt that if small guide books could be obtained at the different ports on route, as well as on board, such as venture would pay handsomely and increase the pleasure of the voyage, and be an interesting memorial. If this idea were carried out, it would not only be appreciated by the passengers, but would be in the best interests of the Company itself.

I purchased half a dozen, silk embroidered, ladies' pocket handkerchiefs for 8/- and half a dozen gentlemen's of the same quality, but of larger size, for 12/-. We got away about 6 p.m. and later in the evening I wrote to my sister Mrs. Dodds.

Saturday October 19th (9th day).

There was nothing of interest today till about noon, when we entered the Straits of Bonifacio. It was here the passengers on the *Ormuz* were vaccinated on July 15 when

---

[105] From the description, this must be the Fort Saint-Jean.

Chapter 4

on our voyage to England. No towns were seen, and the coasts were destitute of vegetation. A poor little robin has been flying around the boat all day, how it got so far from land and what became of it, are questions easier to ask than solved.

Sent letter and post card to my English friends, as here stated. Post cards:— Rev. F.W. Langton my nephew, George Dodds, my Uncle Willie, Fred Farmeloe.

Position 41° 18' N, 9° 16' E. Run from Marseilles 228 miles.

Sunday October 20th (10th day).

Arrived at Naples at daylight, and anchored about half a mile from the town, and were soon surrounded by the usual fleet of small boats, each bringing their different wares to be disposed of. The City is beautiful for situation, and when viewed from the sea, is a sight not very easily forgotten. Five of us – Messrs. Gilbertson, MacDonald, Bate, Jaques and myself, went ashore and engaged a guide who for 16/- each, engaged to conduct us through the King's Church, The Royal Palace, The Royal Museum, and The Ruins of Pompeii.

First we were taken through the principal streets in a comfortable four wheeled conveyance drawn by two horses. The streets are wide and well kept, flanked by noble buildings and the monuments are chaste in design and execution. The suburban residences are well built and spacious, and as a large number are on the slopes of Vesuvius, it gives the city the appearance of being what it really is – "a City set on a hill, which cannot be hid."[106] Another thing worthy of remark is the number of trees, both fruit and ornamental, that abound on every hand, but these being principally in the gardens, and often through an archway, are not seen to advantage. The day was fine and the sky beautifully clear, so I think we saw the city at its best.

But there is another side to the picture that I hesitate to give, although it ought to be told. In the poorer portion of the town, the streets are much narrower, have no sidewalks, and are strewn with garbage and filth. The tenements are small and not over clean, and in many of them, the fowls have the run of the floor.

I saw things in Naples today that I dare not repeat, but which convinced me that the morals of the people are reflected in the conditions I am trying to describe. I am more and more convinced the morals of a people cannot be gauged by the number of their churches, shrines and priests. Here the priests swarm in the street and the churches are amongst the most beautiful in the world, and as you travel along the road in the vicinity of the city, the shrines, or resting places, are found in plenty.

I conclude from what I have seen here that the morals of the people are in an inverse ratio to the number of priests. I was amazed to see the number of men in clerical uniform and I don't wonder that Italy is cursed with poverty. "What I have written, I have nought exaggerated, or nought set down in malice."

---

[106] King James bible, Matthew 5:14.

Chapter 4

Figure 57 Street scene in Naples in 1903. (H.C. White Co., Library of Congress, item LC-USZ62-73723).

We went next to the Royal Museum, said to the best in Europe. We passed through the various Statuary Halls, in which are placed the marbles and bronzes from Herculaneum and Pompeii. The bronze figures were small though remarkably chaste, while those in marble being generally life size, had suffered far more severely from the fiery ordeal through which they had passed. The subjects exhibited in this section are beyond my criticism. Those most admired were the "Bull and his Captors", "The dying gladiator", "Apollo and his lyre", and a carved "Sarcophagus" from Pompeii. We then entered a room in which were exhibited several paintings taken from the City.

Returning to New Zealand in 1901

The figures seemed to be absolutely perfect in features, poise, and colour. We were assured that the pigments used at the time, cannot now be produced.

And let me say again what I have seen today that I am more than ever convinced the moral conduct of the people cannot be gauged by the number of its religious institutions, the number of its clergy or its magnificent churches. The never failing test, by which any religious institution is worthy of being held in remembrance, is what it has *done*.

Here was an interesting relic of what might have come from the Stock Exchange of this old city. It consisted of a square block of marble, and on the top side were three basins about six inches in diameter scooped out each about the size of a pint basin, and in these we were told the brokers kept their change. There was also a Roman Calendar, that stood about two feet high, and each of its four faces measuring about twelve inches across, was divided into three columns, each representing one month, the names of the months being somewhat similar to those now in use.

There was a collection of old, lead waterpipes, marble baths; a pillar from The Court House, three cases of pigment, used by the artists of that day, and a room, floored in mosaic with marble cubes about half an inch in size, in which every figure and tree were beautifully reproduced by the small marble cubes as just stated. From the museum, we were taken to the church of St. Januarius, popularly known as the King's Church. I was not able to get the dimensions, but I supposed it would be about the size of St. Paul's in London, and similar in design.

CHAPTER 4

Divine service was going on, but there were far more sightseers than worshipers, not more than fifty being present, and these seemed to be in no way inconvenienced. The service (or what I suppose was regarded as such) was conducted by an aged priest clad in gorgeous vestments and seemed to consist in the worshippers following him from one part of the building to another, he carrying a book, and they walking in an orderly way. I did not expect to understand his language, but I did not even hear the sound of his voice. In other parts of the church some were kneeling and counting their beads, but were in no way interested in the public worship that was going on

The friezes that adorn the side panels and the ceiling, are said to be the work of Murillo, and exceeded in beauty anything of the kind I had seen. Sculptured figures of saints and evangelists, considerably over life size, were placed at intervals around the interior of the building.

More than twenty domes could be counted as we lay at anchor in the roadstead, but that of the King's Church is by far the largest in Naples and at night, when lighted up, it is a magnificent spectacle. St. Januarius, the patron saint, was bishop of Benevents in the 3rd century and suffered martyrdom under Diocletian A.D. 305. His anniversary is on the 19th of September, on which day two phials of his blood, preserved in the church at Naples are said to possess the power of liquefaction, and are carried in procession. Today not being September 19th, we missed the interesting spectacle.

The King's Palace, which stands just opposite the Church we have been considering, next claimed our attention, and seen from the outside does not present a very attractive appearance. It is old, weather-beaten, and dingy, but this is forgotten and more than atoned for when the threshold has been crossed. All the staircases, are of polished marble and not less than from ten to twelve feet wide. The first apartment that we entered was the ball room, which is eighty feet square, and the walls are hung with pictures by the great masters. It is lighted by five immense chandeliers, that in the centre being twelve feet in diameter and holds eighty candles, the four corner lights are each nine feet in diameter and hold sixty candles each. The dining room is eighty feet square, and the floor is laid with veined terra-cotta and the furniture is upholstered in French-grey silk.

The King's private chapel is elaborate in its furnishings and appointments, and is also upholstered with French-grey silk. Here and in the King's Church the ceiling is frescoed with paintings by Murillo. The altar is of polished Malachite with marble pillars, either of white Carrara, or veined Oriental. His Majesty's private theatre is equally beautiful. The King's box is immediately in front of the stage and is draped with curtains of scarlet and gold. The Dining Room Diplomatic, is in general character with the rooms referred to, except that the floor is panelled with satinwood, the framing being made with wood of a darker hue.

The Throne Room is the most gorgeous of all. The walls are draped with beautiful paintings and Gobelin tapestry, one of the latter representing Neptune's court measures twenty feet by sixteen feet. Here the old sea-god is seen sitting in his chariot-drawn by four dolphins, and attended by fabulous sea monsters, triton and nymphs. On the same wall was

Chapter 4

another piece of tapestry, the same size as the former, but I was unable to get the title, and we passed so quickly through the room that I had no time to memorise what I saw. I thought the throne itself looked a little shabby, when compared with its surroundings. It resembled neither more or less, than a large gilded armchair, and was merely standing on the floor. The balcony at the front overlooked the King's gardens while that at the back overlooked the courtyard, which lay far below. Treasures from Pompeii were set up in all directions and all the rooms, except the dining room, were richly carpeted.

After leaving the Palace we were taken along the Vesuvius Road to Pompeii, which lies 14 miles South East of Naples. The town of Pompeii was destroyed by an eruption of Mount Vesuvius A.D. 79 and its site was not rediscovered till 1748. After lunch at the Vesuvius Hotel we proceeded to view the famous ruins.

On the right as you enter the museum, lies a dog, crumpled up as though in its death agony, and on the left you see a little babe, who had lain in its bed of ashes for nearly two thousand years. Along the centre of the museum, are series of glass cases each containing a mummified specimen of humanity. Here lies a lady who had probably been killed while she fled, one hand is held across her forehead as though to protect her from the falling storm of stones and mud.

Here are the remains of strong men, whose features are still quite recognizable, and in some the teeth are still white and apparently in good order and in every case the skull is in a fair state of preservation, and the bone in the fingers of the clenched fist, plainly seen. In one case lie the bodies of mother and daughter, they are joined together at the hips what seems to be a band of consolidated love about four inches wide, some think they died together as they slept, and others that they were struck down as they fled for safety.

Figure 58 Pompeii at about the time when Thomas saw it. (Photographer: William Henry Goodyear 1846–1923, Brooklyn Museum archives, item S03 06 01 024, from Wikipedia).

In other cases, placed on shelves around the museum are innumerable specimens of lamps, pitchers, and bronze ornaments of various sorts. Here are loaves, taken from the oven in which they were baking when the fiery rain came down upon the devoted town, they are same size and shape of those we saw in the bakers' shops today, they are circular; about ten inches in diameter and an inch and a half thick,

Chapter 4

and have a two inch circular hole in the centre, by which they are hung up.

We then visited the ruins, which are in a wonderful scale of preservation. In many places the paved and raised sidewalks are in the same condition as prior to the great calamity that destroyed the town. The streets are paved with blocks of stone about two feet square, and in many instances these are worn into ruts – not with modern traffic for there is none today, but with that two thousand years ago. In what had been one of the principal streets the line of buildings on each side is almost continuous, though as might be expected the height varies greatly. In some places, six or eight inches is only the height of the remaining portion, and in another place the wall may be standing nearly up to the original height. Columns that had been part of some building were left standing, while only a few feet away, every little trace of the original wall was to be seen. When in position these noble columns would appear to be composed of solid marble, but in their present condition it could now be seen that the centre portion was filled in with brick and cement, the outside only being marble. The streets we traversed, were not more than nine feet between the kerbing on each side, and how the traffic was regulated, is a puzzle that none of our party could solve.

Here is a wine shop, in which are still three jars that were in use when the city flourished, and at no great distance is another, where the jars are more numerous and in better condition.

From what is left of the theatre, it appears to have been a most extensive building, columns that had formed a part of the original building are left standing, but of the remainder, little is left. The building had been semi-circular in shape, and wide stone platforms rose in succession from side to side from the floor almost to the ceiling. The proscenium occupied the entire width of the building, and a large number of fluted columns, many of them with their curved capitals still intact, stood in line where the front of the building had been.

We next paid a visit to the soldiers' barracks, the square being plainly marked off by the rows of marble pillars that had formerly supported the building. At no great distance from the barracks, are the cells in which the criminals were confined, and in close proximity to the entrance the concrete block, on which the guilty were executed.

The paintings on the walls are still plainly seen, several of them being in a remarkable state of preservation. In one apartment, is a beautiful fountain done in mosaic. The floor is of white marble, and the various figures are done in stone of different colours, and each stone only about half an inch square. A little farther on we came to the bakehouse in which the oven and the hand-mills were found to be in a wonderful state of preservation.

Some of the paintings cannot be described, but they testify to the low state of morals then existing.[107]

And thus we walked up street after street, until the time drew near for our return to Naples. On our way to town, we

---

[107] Perhaps Thomas is referring to the mural in the *Terme Suburbane*. It depicts a wide range of intimate acts, many of which would have been criminal offences in 1901.

CHAPTER 4

had a near view of Vesuvius, which was clearly seen from base to summit. I think I have never been more deeply impressed than by what I have seen at Pompeii today.

Got to Naples at 7 p.m. Wrote to Sallie, Susannah and Lil.

Monday October 21st (11th day).

Left Naples at 4 a.m. and have been going along the Italian coast all day, we passed Stromboli during the forenoon, when a dense cloud of smoke was issuing from the crater. There is a lighthouse on the western coast of the island and on the eastern end, are a number of small rocky islets. Towards evening we were passing through the straits of Messina. In one place the channel is only about a mile wide, and nowhere does it seem to be more than two or three, and no more beautiful scenery is to witnessed on the voyage. The hills on both sides of the straits are devoted to vine growing, and pretty little villages nestle on the banks. We had a good view of Messina as we passed. The city is built at the foot of the hill, though several scattered houses are on the slopes beyond; it has a fine harbour, and the population is about one hundred and forty thousand. On the Italian side, and a little farther to the south, is the town of Reggio with a population of forty thousand.

At noon our position was 39° 25' N, 15° 6' E. Run from Naples 96 miles.

Tuesday October 22nd (12th day).

The wind blew hard all night, and today the sea has been a little choppy, and several passengers are suffering from seasickness. I am evidently a better sailor than when on the outward voyage, as I have not suffered in that way during this trip.

The ship's position was not posted today.

Wednesday October 23rd (13th day).

All going well. The sea smooth, the weather delightful, and the boat steady. Wrote to Mr. J. B. Bowes and Martin Jameson.

Thursday October 24th (14th day).

About noon we came in sight of the shipping lying in the harbour of Alexandria and the light, on what appeared to be a tongue of land lying a little farther towards the west, possibly this may be the Isle of Pharos on which Ptolemy built the first lighthouse 300 years B.C. and when we saw these landmarks we knew we were nearing Port Said, and almost before we lost sight of the former the latter appeared ahead, where we arrived at 1.30, and as we were tying up the coal barges came alongside and coaling began. They are the same chattering, hardworking crowd we met on our voyage to England. The poor wretches are to be pitied for they are badly used. I saw one of them get an unmerciful ropes-ending, but I could never find out what he had done to deserve it.

Chapter 4

I did not go ashore, for I saw nothing that appealed to me in that direction, and with the aid of my field-glass I could see all I desired. Port Said is not a town in the ordinary sense of the term, but just a succession of wharves, warehouses, and shipping offices.

Figure 59 Port Said in 1900. (Photographer: unknown, Dr. Paula Sanders collection, Rice University).

There are few houses to be seen, and we wondered where the people live, the governmental element is so preponderating that the domestic is dwarfed into insignificance. There were the usual number of Arab dhows, large ocean steamers, and ocean tramps. It seemed home-like to see The *Jupiter* from Hartlepool and the *Fernglen* from Newcastle lying at the wharf. Coaling was finished by 6.30 p.m. and at 7.15 p.m. we got away and were soon in the canal. It is now eleven p.m. and we are running dead slow owing to other vessels being ahead of us.

Our run today was 356 miles.

Position not given.

Returning to New Zealand in 1901

Friday October 25th (15th day).

Arrived at Suez at 12:40 a.m. We saw more land today than when on voyage to England (see July 9th) some of the stations looked very well, being surrounded by tropical trees of various sorts. Several Arabs were loitering about and a few camels and bullocks were grazing here and there, but vegetables were few and sand too plentiful. Some native youths ran along the bank for miles being enticed by the passengers who threw them coppers as they ran. One fellow, who was the tallest and thinnest, had the longest legs of any in the pack, and the antics of this member of the team caused a great deal of amusement. Though all the coins fell either in the water or on the sand, I am convinced that nearly all were discovered by our dusky friends.

The *Ortona* did not stop at Suez, but steamed very slowly while mails were being transhipped, and when we had travelled about three miles dropped anchor for half an hour to unship the false rudder that we used in the Canal, and then full speed for Colombo. We left Suez about 6.30 and have been steaming down the Gulf since that time. The night is clear, and as the moon is shining brightly we can see the land as plainly as in daylight. It is now 8.30, and we are passing the unsightly lighthouse on Cape Ashraf. HMS *Crecy* was lying at Suez as we passed.

Later 11 p.m. The day has been insufferably hot, and I have discarded my body flannel and under pants and other superficial clothing; several passengers are sleeping on deck.

The Red Sea extends 1400 miles from The Indian Ocean, and varies width, from 20 to 200 miles. The Canal was

Chapter 4

opened in 1869 and is 99 miles long. The cost at the time of opening was £12,000,000. By the purchase of the Khedive's shares in 1875 Britain became the controlling power. The canal shortens the distance between London and Bombay by about 24 days.

Saturday October 26th (16th day).

When I came on deck this morning the *Ortona* was opposite the Island of Shadwan. It lies very low, and I could see no sign of vegetation. There is a lighthouse on the island, but no houses were visible. At 2 p.m. we met the *Ormuz*, she was again on her voyage to England and at that time I was anticipating a three months sojourn in the Homeland. At 2.30 we passed a solitary lighthouse, standing like a beacon in the solitary waste of water, and like the Eddystone it seemed to rise from out of the sea, but I was unable to obtain its name.

The weather continues intensely hot, and today the remainder of the ship's awnings have been set, and the shade is most welcome.

Position at noon 25° 21' N, 35° 37' E. Run 322 miles.

Sunday October 27th (17th day).

Heat most oppressive, otherwise the weather is beautiful. We have seen neither land or ship today. An owl, a wagtail, and a swallow have been flying round the ship all day, the latter came on board and was welcomed, but after resting a while he took his departure. A Church of England service was held on board; we met in the first class compartment, and it was conducted by the Rev. Mr. Hart, one of the first class passengers whose text was Psalm XIX, verse I, "The heavens declare the glory of God, and the firmament showeth his handywork." It was a good sermon, and most appropriate as there was a partial eclipse of the moon, while the service was being held.

Position 20° 12' N, 38° 43' E. Distance run 353 miles.

Monday October 28th (18th day).

This afternoon we passed the group of small islands known as the Twelve Apostles, and at dusk we were entering the Straits of Babelmandeb, and a little later we passed the island of Perim, which though comparatively near we did not see. We are now in the Arabian Gulf and our course is nearly due east. HMS *Crecy* has been following in our wake since we left Suez but is still a good distance astern. Wrote letters as follows. Mrs. Forester, (née Bessie Moorhead), Annie Boiston, and my cousin Tom.

Position at noon 15° 14' N, 41° 57' E. Run 352 miles.

Tuesday October 29th (19th day).

The weather and sea are all that could be desired, HMS *Crecy* parted company from us this afternoon she going apparently to Aden. A solitary flying-fish and the wide ocean is all we have seen outside the ship today, but nothing worthy of note has taken place.

Wrote to my brother Jack.

Position at noon 12° 11' N, 46° 3' E. Run 340 miles.

CHAPTER 4

Wednesday October 30th (20th day).

We passed Cape Guardafui at noon, and a little later we were opposite the island of Sochatra. This island belongs to Britain, and it commands the entrance to the Arabian Gulf. Although small it is of great strategic importance. Later we passed two islands, known as The Brothers. We are now in the Indian Ocean, and we are told that we may not see land again till we arrive at Colombo on Monday.

Position 12° 1' N, 51° 50' E. Run 341 miles.

Thursday October 31st (21st day).

Neither land or sail today. The only thing that interested was a waterspout similar to the one we saw in the Mediterranean on October 17th and need not again be described. Today we had flying fish in great abundance. The first sports we have had came off today, but they were very uninteresting.

The following table will be of interest.

Miles Travelled		Miles yet to Travel	
Newcastle to Cadiz	300	Colombo to Freemantle	3140
Cadiz to Plymouth	294	Freemantle to Adelaide	1380
Plymouth to Gibralter	1049	Adelaide to Melbourne	499
Gibralter to Marseilles	694	Melbourne to Sydney	596
Marseilles to Naples	456	Sydney to Wellington	1200
Naples to Port Said	1111	Wellington to Napier	212
Port Said to Suez	87		
Suez to Colombo	3402		
	7393		7027

Figure 60 Table of distances from Thomas's diary. (Laws Family Collection).

250

Position at noon 9° 51' N, 63° 11' E. Run 314 miles.

Friday November 1st (22nd day).

The completion of the sports began yesterday, but were as stale, flat, and unprofitable as sports could possibly be.
Position 9° 51' N, 63° 11' E. Run 314 miles.

Saturday November 2nd (23rd day).

The wind blew from the NE this morning and was accompanied by heavy rain, and as the boat rolled considerably things became unpleasant, but during the afternoon the wind ceased, and the sea went down considerably.

I am trying to take three small pot plants home: a Maiden Hair Fern, given me by my cousin Tom, a Campanula, given me by my uncle Willie, and a cutting of one Mr. Cunnold's choice flowers, of which I have no particulars.

We have not seen either ship or land today.

Sunday November 3rd (24th day).

We are trying to overhaul one of the German Lloyd steamers which, like ourselves, is making for Colombo, we can just see her on the horizon, and we appear to be gaining upon her.

Messrs. Bate, Gilbertson, and I stood a long time on deck admiring the brilliant phosphorescence emitted by a species of jelly-fish, of which we see thousands by day, but tonight after dusk their lights were seen to advantage. They studded the sea like stars in the sky on a frosty night, and at other times they seemed to be drawn into contact and formed large patches of shimmering water, only again to be broken up by the vessel as she proceeded on her way making the sea appear like a cauldron of boiling silver.

We had Divine service again at 11 a.m. and 7.30 p.m. Posted letters to my brother Jack, my sister Sallie, and Mr. Coulthard.

Position at noon 7° 55' N, 74° 23' E. Distance run 331 miles.

Figure 61 Colombo harbour in about 1900. (Plâté and Co., Robert Laws Collection).

Monday November 4th (25th day).

Arrived at Colombo at 11 a.m., and as soon as the boat was moored, Messrs. Bate, Brown and I went ashore, and after spending a little time in looking round the principal streets we engaged a trap, the driver agreeing to take us to several places agreed upon at the rate of 5/- each. He first

Returning to New Zealand in 1901

took us along the Galle Face Road, by way of the Galle Face Hotel, the Jubilee Gardens, and the museum. Here there were many interesting exhibits, mostly of Indian origin such as snakes, scorpions, lizards and other reptiles, there were leopards, tigers, monkeys, elephants, and other small animals. There was a fine collections of shells, one monster resembling the shell of an oyster that measured 3ft 6in diameter. There was also a collection of old guns, swords, and native weapons as well as native dresses, bracelets, bangles, and other adornments of a like nature. I was especially interested in the skeleton of an Indian elephant. which was said to have been eight feet high, placed alongside was one of the elephants hoofs, which measured 15 inches across, and it is said that the skeleton and hoof represent the largest elephant ever known.

We then went to the Bhuddist temple. Leaving our carriage at the foot of the hill, and walking about two hundred yards through a grove of trees we came to the temple and were received by the custodian – a young man of about 24 years, and after paying him our fee he took us inside and became our instructor. He was very painstaking, very voluble, and seemed inclined to magnify his office.

The building was all upon the ground floor, severely plain, heavy, built in concrete and whitewashed. The compartments were small and dingy and without the least attempt at ornamentation.

In the first apartment we entered were images of Bhudda in different positions, standing, reclining, and sitting, each in a large glass case that stood about two feet above the floor,

CHAPTER 4

and in front of these was the altar, which was strewn with flowers representing the offerings of the faithful.

In the next compartment, were seven large and two small images of Bhudda and a fairly large image of Vishnu, the latter being much superior to the other in style and finish. In another compartment were representation of heaven and hell showing the punishment that will be metred out for such sin and covetousness, disobedience to parents, drunkenness, theft, and other sins. The virtues, each with its future state of bliss were represented in like manner.

Our guide took great pains to impress upon us the fact that all the works of art we had seen, were the work of native Bhuddists, and this I am certain he accomplished. While not professing to be judge of works of art. The drawings seemed to me to be unnatural and out of proportion, and the colouring worse than the poorest German print. No doubt they appeal to the native mind, and in this way they serve a useful purpose. A small patch of floor in one of the rooms was laid in mosaic, which is composed of small pieces of pottery, and is fairly creditable, though not to be compared with those we saw at Pompeii.

We were shown another building with a heavy, low roof, that our guide told us was The Palace, but whether of priest or monarch he did not say, nor did we ask for further information. There was the usual number of cadgers, dealers in lace, precious stones, prayers, flowers and all such things as are offered for sale at Eastern Ports.

After leaving the temple, we were next taken to Point Lavinia where at present is a camp of Boer prisoners. There are two such camps in Ceylon, Mount Lavinia being the smaller of the two, but were unable to learn the number of prisoners. When we arrived we found quite a number of carriages and rickshaws drawn up at the Lavinia hotel, but without time we started for the camp and went inside. I would not have been surprised to find it surrounded by a brick wall seven or eight feet high, but we found no such barrier to our progress and so went boldly forward, neither did we see a sentry, or any one to keep the prisoners in safe custody. [108]

The buildings are large, clean, and well ventilated and all the manual work is by coolie labour, also the cooking. The day was hot, and few of the prisoners were outside, there were a few however, who were loitering about outside. All appeared to be well-fed, healthy and contented. The camp is surrounded on three sides by cocoa-nut trees and a few other varieties, and in front is Point Lavinia Railway station, the Hotel, and the sea. A more healthy station could not well be found, and apart from having lost their liberty for the present I don't think they had anything to complain about.

It was while we were here we first heard of Colonial Benson's defeat and death, and asking the sergeant if the prisoners knew anything about it, or the war then going on, we were told they got their letters and newspapers regularly and knew as much about the war as did the general public.

As already stated, we were under the impression that the camp was open to the public, but the sergeant told us this was not so and that visitors were not allowed inside the red

---

[108] Mount Lavinia was a *convalescent* camp for Boer prisoners. It was opened on 17 December 1900.

flags, which he pointed out to us, and which we now noticed for the first time. So there was nothing for us to do but to apologize for our intrusion, and take our departure, but had it not been for our mistake, we would not have seen so much, or received so much information.

We got back to Colombo about 4 p.m., and I am more than ever impressed with the beauty of the city and its surroundings. The tropical foliage, with its depth of colour, the size of the flowers, the endless profusion of coconut, bread-fruit, cinnamon and peppers and other tropical trees, the beautiful lake, and the Singalese themselves, all conspire to make Colombo a delightful and lasting memory. I purchased a few presents for those friends I left in Napier five months ago: three embroidered table covers, each about three feet square for 8/- and one of larger size and better quality for 12/-.

On our way to the wharf we passed the Mohammedan temple[109], there is nothing chaste either in design or construction. Its front is covered with carved figures – human, animal, and mythical. The door was wide open and though not allowed to enter, we stood on the opposite side of the street, and we had a good view of the interior, but there was nothing to see that is worthy of remark. Two men, apparently on guard, stood at the entrance, while gongs were beaten and other disagreeable noises were being made by those inside, but there was no attempt at music of any kind.

---

[109] This was probably the Murugan *Hindu* temple.

The little children at Colombo, are the prettiest and the most winsome I have seen anywhere (except in Enfield Road or Munroe Street, Napier).

We got back to the *Ortona* at 6.45 p.m. but it was not till 10 p.m. that the screws began to revolve that the last of our dusky compatriots lowered himself over the ship's side and took his departure. Lovely Colombo, my thoughts will often stray to thee after reaching my own dear home from the distant East.

Our run from noon yesterday to Colombo was 331 miles.

Tuesday November 5th (26th day).

Heavy rain this morning; this being the rainy season we may expect this kind of weather while in the tropics. About 10:30 the rain ceased and the remainder of the day was blazing hot. The run between Colombo and Fremantle is the least interesting part of our journey, and generally about ten days long. We saw no land and very little shipping. The only thing we are likely to see in plenty is the water we are passing through.

During the forenoon a young stowaway was found coiled up under a tarpaulin. He appears to be about twelve years of age, and came from Colombo. He is now peeling potatoes, and he will have to make himself generally useful while on board and will probably be shipped home from Fremantle.

Position at noon 4° 25' N, 81° 11' E. Run 181 miles.

Chapter 4

Wednesday November 6th (27th day).

Heavy rain from early morning till 3 p.m. The sea has been remarkably calm, just like a sea of glass. We crossed the equator at 12.41 p.m., and we are now in the southern hemisphere, our position at noon being 0° 5' S, 8° 12' E. Run 181 miles.

Thursday November 7th (28th day).

Heavy rain, almost continuous, and there has also been a choppy sea. Owing to some neglect, the position of the ship has not been given today.

Friday November 8th (29th day).

Heavy rain all day and also a heavy sea.

Someone has either taken or destroyed the Campanula given me by my dear old uncle, and which I was trying to get safely to New Zealand. I put it outside at 6.30 and the last I saw of it was when called to breakfast at 8 a.m., but at 8.30 it was gone. I am of the opinion that some of the sailors pitched it overboard when washing the decks. I don't think any one of them would care sufficiently about flowers to steal it, but some of them would glory in such an act of petty annoyance. I am sorry to lose it, and it was getting so nicely after having travelled so far.

Position at noon 81° 13' S, 92° 38' E. Run 337 miles.

Saturday November 9th (30th day).

Strong head wind and heavy sea, with a good deal of seasickness among the passengers. Land was seen on our left, but it is not marked on any map to which I have access. Wrote to my dear uncle Willie.

Position at noon 11° 58' S, 96° 12' E. Run 312 miles.

Sunday November 10th (31st day).

Wind still high, though not so bad as yesterday. At noon the sun is almost vertical and consequently at that time our bodies cast no shadow, or to be more correct, the shadow we possess is under our feet. We met one of the French mail boats, but I could not get her name.

Monday November 11th (32nd day).

This has been a weary day, nothing has been seen outside the boat except a few flying fish and the *Ortona* has rolled terribly. Just after dinner she gave a fearful lurch, accompanied by a great noise, and being on deck at the time I went down below to investigate and found that piles of crockery, which the stewards were about to wash, had been thrown down, and there had been a great slaughter among the plates and dishes, and a large tub of slops had been capsized "and great was the mess thereof."

Wrote to Charlie.

Position 20° 4' S, 104° 6' E. Run 353 miles.

CHAPTER 4

Tuesday November 12th (33rd day).

Today the weather has been worse than we had it yesterday. We have not even seen a flying fish, and the boat has rolled heavily, but I am thankful to say we have made a good run, and that compensates us for the unpleasantness referred to.

Position at noon 24° 46' S, 108° 16' E. Run 354 miles.

Wednesday November 13th (34th day).

Sea moderate, weather calm with a cutting southerly blowing. The sailors are preparing for the discharge of cargo at Fremantle tomorrow, where we expect to arrive early. Spent some time tonight in trying to locate the Southern Cross, but did not succeed.

Position at noon 29° 8' S, 112° 35' E. Run 350 miles, and distance from Fremantle 239 miles.

Thursday November 14th (35th day).

When we awoke this morning we found that we were moored at Fremantle, and after breakfast Mr. Brown and I had a look through the town. I would have gone to Perth and called on my wife's brother, Mr. J. Newlands, but there was not sufficient time to take to journey. Fremantle is not a nice town, but being the port for the whole district of Western Australia, a large amount of business is done. A number of steamers and also sailing vessels, were lying at the wharf, and several large warehouses were in the immediate vicinity. The streets are clean and in good order, but too narrow for a town with such a prospect before it.

Figure 62 Fremantle in 1900. (Photographer: unknown, State Library of Western Australia, item slwa_b1967237_9).

When we left England, a little over a month ago, harvest was over, and most of the fruit had been gathered, a few late tomatoes were grown under glass and were still obtainable, but they were of poor quality, and everything pointed to the approach of winter. Today, I find myself in a different hemisphere, where it is glorious summer. The shops are full of produce, peas, beans, early potatoes, French beans, and other vegetables being abundant.

A number of passengers left the boat here, and several joined for other parts of Western Australia. We left at noon and now 8 p.m. we are off Cape Leeuwin. Got letters from Eva and Mr. W. H. Newlands.

CHAPTER 4

Friday November 15th (36th day).

Weather cold and dull, sea smooth. We passed Albany in the night and have since been steaming along the Australian Coast, and at 6 p.m. we were entering the Great Australian Bight. Nothing of interest to record.

Position 35° 9' S, 117° 46' E. Run 326 miles.

Saturday November 16th (37th day).

Nothing of interest today, except it be that half a dozen albatross have been following us since early morning, they are much smaller than those we saw when coming to New Zealand in 1873. At 4 p.m. we sighted Orient *Cuzco* on her way to England and as I write 8 p.m., we are about half way through the Great Australian Bight.

Mr. Brown and I stood for a good while this morning watching the gambols of a school of porpoises that were playing at the bow of the boat. The last of the concerts was given last night. I need to say that previous concerts have not reached a professional standard, but let us not forget that it was said of one in New Testament times "She hath done what she could" and the same may be said of those who have endeavoured to lighten the deadly dullness of along sea voyage, and both committee and performers are worthy of the vote of thanks they received.

Position 35° 19' S, 124° 97' E. Run 334 miles.

Sunday November 17th (38th day).

A heavy swell and the ship rolling a good deal otherwise the day has been fine; we are now getting well through the Bight, and we hope to reach Adelaide about noon tomorrow. Attended Divine service at 7.30 p.m. when Mr. Hart preached from Deut. xxxiii, 27, "The eternal God is thy refuge, and underneath are the everlasting arms", I have not been able to find out, to what particular denomination he belongs, but he is a good preacher, quite orthodox according to our Methodist standards, and I doubt not is a good Christian man.

Position 35° 19' S, 124° 9' E. Run 342 miles.

Monday November 18th (39th day).

Came on deck at 6.30 and found that we are opposite to Kangaroo Island. It is 80 miles long, with an average width of 20 miles, and from this time till we arrive at Port Adelaide we had land on both sides. Here we discharge all the mails for Adelaide and several passengers too. The town is built on a narrow slip of land at the foot of the hills. The town as seen from the anchorage is long and narrow, and the buildings are very plain. The river Torrence [*sic*] runs a short distance from the coast and about parallel with it and is navigable for small craft for about 12 miles. We left for Melbourne at 7.30 p.m.

CHAPTER 4

Tuesday November 19th (40th day).

We have going along the Australian coast all day. Mr. Brown and I stood for a long time on the forecastle-head, watching a number of porpoises that were playing at the bow. The passengers who are leaving the boat at Melbourne, are gathering up their loose luggage and packing their trunks in view of leaving the boat tomorrow, we expect to get into port about 6 a.m. The last of the concerts was given tonight. The committee, have done their best for us with the material at their disposal and they deserve our warmest thanks.

Position 38° 4' S, 140° 27' E. Run 244 miles.

Wednesday November 20th (41st day).

Arrived at Melbourne at 7 a.m., and before the boat was made fast we were examined by the health officers and declared to be free from disease. For some time, there was a scene of wild confusion as people went about the deck with their luggage, and the customs examining boxes and other receptacles, and all the time, the stevedores working cargo, and as soon as possible I went ashore.

I had brought two books and a letter from Mrs. Donald of Edinburgh who by-the-way is the mother of Mr. Smalley – the mother or our first Napier minister. These I delivered and then went to Flinders Street, where I met my brother in law, Mr. Edgar Newlands and had a long talk with him about family matters, and after a cup of tea with him he returned to Castlemaine and I to the *Ortona*. I got on board at 5 p.m. and found the boat almost deserted, though cargo was still being discharged, but a large number of passengers had left, and those who were proceeding to Sydney had not returned from their excursion to town.

Mr. Edgar Newlands gave me two curious plants known as Stag's horns – a parasite that grows on trees in the Australian bush – I hope to get them safely to New Zealand.

Late in the evening we had quite a Saturnalia on board, many who had been on board, returned under the influence of liquor and more was obtained after arriving on board, the result being such a pandemonium as I have no desire to witness again. Drinking, swearing, and fighting were freely indulged in until after midnight.

Messrs. Bate and Gilbertson, my now best chums, were among those who disembarked today. Left for Sydney at midnight.

Thursday November 21st (42nd day).

Fine weather and a smooth sea. So many left the boat at Melbourne that her deck seems now to be deserted. I was told a few days ago the Napier passengers would be sent on from Sydney by the *Talune*, leaving on Saturday November 23rd at 1 p.m., and that statement is confirmed by a notice on board to that effect. The New Zealand passengers, numbering about 30 in all, are all that are now left on board.

Saw three whales this afternoon, the one being nearest the boat spouted several times.

Position 38° 56' S, 146° 55E. Run from Melbourne 168 miles.

Chapter 4

Figure 63 The SS *Talune*. Thomas sailed on her from Sydney to Wellington. (Photographer: David Alexander De Maus 1847–1925, Port Chalmers Regional Museum, from Wikipedia).

Friday November 22nd (43rd day).

We continued our course along the Australian coast till 3 p.m., when Sydney Heads was sighted at 4.20 we entered the harbour, said to be the best in the world, it is full of picturesque nooks and bays and in many places the banks are covered with shrubbery down to the water's edge. Beautiful villa residences are scattered along the shore and on the rising ground beyond.

Shortly after being tied up all passengers' luggage was sent ashore, and the Queensland passengers were also taken off and will proceed to their destination tonight. The New Zealanders, numbering about thirty, being all that are now left on board. Mr. Brown and I left our former quarters and took our luggage to the after part of the boat where we intend to sleep.

Now that very few passengers are left, I say in all seriousness, there are not more than a dozen that I would go out my way to meet again. To be compelled to mix with such characters, as have been my shipmates during the last six weeks, is almost enough to make one despair of their regeneration.

Saturday November 23rd (44th day).

Slept on deck, but as the lumpers began coaling for the return journey at 3 a.m. there was neither sleep or rest after that hour so we rose early and had the satisfaction of seeing the harbour at its best. The sun rose in an unclouded sky. The trees had put on their beautiful garments and I was nearing home.

At 10 a.m. I bid good bye to the *Ortona,* and the New Zealand passengers and their luggage were taken to the New Zealand Company's office where I got my ticket for Wellington and booked my luggage by the *Talune*. I am sure it will not go by that boat, but will be sent via Auckland by steamer leaving on Wednesday. I naturally assumed it would go by the same boat as myself. I have written to the manager of the Orient line pointing out the position and asking him to do what was necessary to procure the safe arrival of my luggage in Napier. I cannot understand why it should not be sent to Napier in the same boat as myself.

We left at 6 p.m. for what I hope will be the last stage of our long journey and are travelling by the *Talune*. Mr. Brown

Chapter 4

from Dannevirke, who was a chum of mine on our voyage to England on the *Ormuz*, has also been my fellow passenger in the *Ortona*.

Sunday November 24th (45th day).

Spent a miserable and unprofitable day on board the *Talune*. The weather is cold and there is a choppy sea, with a good deal of sea sickness.

Our position at noon was 35° 11' S, 15° 25' E. Run 224 miles.

Monday November 25th (46th day).

Nothing occurred today to relieve the lameness of the journey except it be the overhauling of two steamers and the number of albatross that have been following us. The food and the accommodation are excellent, and superior in both respect to what we got on the *Ortona*.

Position 26° 52' S, 101° 8' E. Run 295 miles.

Tuesday November 26th (47th day).

Very little to record, saw two or three whales and the albatross are still following in our wake.

Position 38° 40' S, 167° 03' E. Run today 300 miles.

Wednesday November 27th (48th day).

Cape Farwell was sighted about 6 a.m. Mount Egmont which seemed to rise from the sea, was covered with snow from the lower slopes to the summit. We steamed along the coast till noon, when we caught a glimpse of Port Nelson. The coast does not appear the same as when on my arrival in New Zealand on Tuesday September 23rd 1873, when I wrote:

> At 4.45, we caught sight of Cape Farewell. The scenery along the coast was magnificent, rising from the foothills with increasing altitude as their distance from the coast increased; and as far as the eye could see, the highest were covered with snow and the most brilliantly tinted clouds.

I saw nothing like this description today, but possibly the same scene was witnessed under different conditions. During the afternoon we entered Cook Strait, and had land on both side of us.

The albatross have left us, and all day we have been followed by a large number of gulls. These birds are either very tame, or very hungry for they are continually alighting on the boat and would fight for a place on the truck at the masthead, and some of them would even perch on the flagstaff at the forecastle head, though fifty passengers were walking about within ten or twelve feet of them.

During the day we passed through several large shoals of fish, in fact the water in patches seemed to be alive with them, I would have said they were mackerel, but there are no mackerel in these seas. We arrived in the roadstead at Napier at 7.30 p.m., but will not be allowed to land till we have passed the health officers tomorrow. The mail however was taken off at nine o'clock and now (10 p.m.) all is excitement on board, and there will be little sleep tonight.

CHAPTER 4

Our position at noon was 40° 30' S, 173° 7' E. Run 304 miles. Distance from Wellington 116 miles and from Sydney 1123 miles.

I am booked to Napier and could travel by first boat, but have decided to leave Wellington by first train on Friday morning.

Thursday November 28th (49th day).

At 6.30 the health officers came on board and after a brief inspection, we proceeded to the wharf, and the first to greet me on arrival was the Rev. C. E. Beecroft, who was in Wellington attending The District meeting. Bertha, who had come from Napier, was on the wharf as soon as Mr. Beecroft, and from both I received a hearty welcome.

After a little delay I got my luggage through the customs, and as Mr. Trevor had very kindly sent his trap, I had my luggage sent to the railway station at Te Aro. After lunch I bought four small pictures, two each for my dear wife and "Millie" my daughter in law and also a hand ball for Dorothy. After tea we had a very pleasant evening. The Revds. C. E. Beecroft and I. Houndsel being present.

Friday November 29th (50th day).

Bertha and I were early astir this morning, having to catch the Napier express (Figure 64). On the platform I met James Brown who had travelled with me on the *Ormuz*, and also on the *Ortona*, and who is now on the way to his home at Dannevirke. I could not help noticing how quickly we were scattering. Brown and I were the only passengers on the train who had been with us on the round trip and now were soon to give each other a parting shake of the hand and say goodbye. Mr. James Ashcroft was looking for me at Dannevirke and Mr. Cunnold at Hastings, and while the train waited at the respective stations I had a few words with each and with other friends.

Figure 64 The Napier Express train travelling over the Mangatera viaduct near Dannevirke. (Photographer: Wilsons, Sir George Grey Special Collections, Auckland Libraries, item 35-R1180).

At 6.50 p.m. we got to Napier, where several of my old friends were waiting my arrival, and I had to do a good deal of hand-shaking, and when this was over I was allowed to go home and end my return journey after an absence of six months.

CHAPTER 4

Figure 65 Thomas happily reunited with his family in Napier. Freddie and Charlie are in the back row, left. (Laws Family Collection).

5. Poetry

Having now completed the journal of my travels to and from the old country to New Zealand. I will now conclude with a few choice pieces of poetry.[110]

The Sailor's Song[111]

The wind blows light, and the day is bright
And the good ship has spread her sails
The sailor sings for her merry-wings,
Have oft come him through stormy gales
Her track must be, to the Northern Sea,
To the region of ice and snow.

A voyage full rough, but the ship is tough.
Nor with fear doth the sailor go
But he sings "keep her free on the open-sea
With her head to the north once more
And the compass our guide, on the ocean wide,
We're as safe as the lubbers on shore."

---

[110] The verses are reproduced here as written by Thomas.

[111] The author is unknown; perhaps Thomas wrote this piece.

Chapter 5

The wind blows strong, and the night is long.
And the ship labours under bare poles
The sailors haul, to the bosun's call
As they sail amid dangerous shoals.
The steersman stands, with his brawny hands
On the spokes of the guiding wheel.

He heaves it around, with a clanking sound
While the ship, to the gale doth heel,
And he sings "keep her free on the open sea
With her head to the north once more
And the compass our guide on the ocean wide
We're as safe as the lubbers on shore."

A year and a day since she sailed away,
And the good ship has never returned,
The Sailor's wife has a sad lone life
But to wait in hope she has learned.
She sits by the door of her cot on the shore
There to gaze on the sea far out.

A ship comes in sight, fills her heart with delight
Soon she hears the glad sailors shout.
As they sing "keep her free on the open sea
With her head to our home once more,
And the compass our guide, on the ocean wide,
We've come back to our friends on shore.

New Zealand National Anthem

God of nations at thy feet
In thy bonds of love we meet
Hear our voices we entreat
God defend our Free Land
Guard Pacific's triple star
From the shafts of strife and war
Make her praises [heard] afar
    God defend New Zealand.

Men of every creed and race
Gather here before thy face
Asking thee to bless this place
God defend our Free Land
From dissention, envy, hate
And corruption guard our state
Make our country good and great
    God defend New Zealand.

Peace not war shall be our boast
But should foes assault our coast
Make us then a mighty host
God defend New Zealand.
Lord of battles in thy might
Put our enemies to flight
Let our cause be just and right
    God defend New Zealand.

Chapter 5

Let our love thee increase
May thy blessing never cease
Give us plenty, give us peace
God defend our Free Land
From dishonour and from shame
Guard our country's spotless name
Crown her with immortal fame.
    God defend New Zealand.

May our mountains ever be,
Freedom's ramparts on the sea
Make us faithful unto thee
    God defend New Zealand.

Guide her in the nations' van
Preaching love and truth to man
Working out thy glorious plan
    God defend New Zealand.

The Little Dog-Angel[112]

High up in the courts of heaven today.
A little dog-angel waits,
With the rest of the angels he will not play
But sits alone at the gates
"For I know that my master will come", says he
"And when he comes he will call for me."

And his master far on the earth below
As he sits in his easy chair
Forgets sometime and he whistles low
For the dog that is not there
And the dear little doggie, cocks his ears
And dreams that his master's voice he hears.

And I know when at length his master waits
Outside in the dark and the cold
For the hand of death to open the gates
That lead to those courts of gold
The little dog angel's eager bark
Will comfort his soul in the shivering dark.

---

[112] by Norah M. Holland (1876–1925).

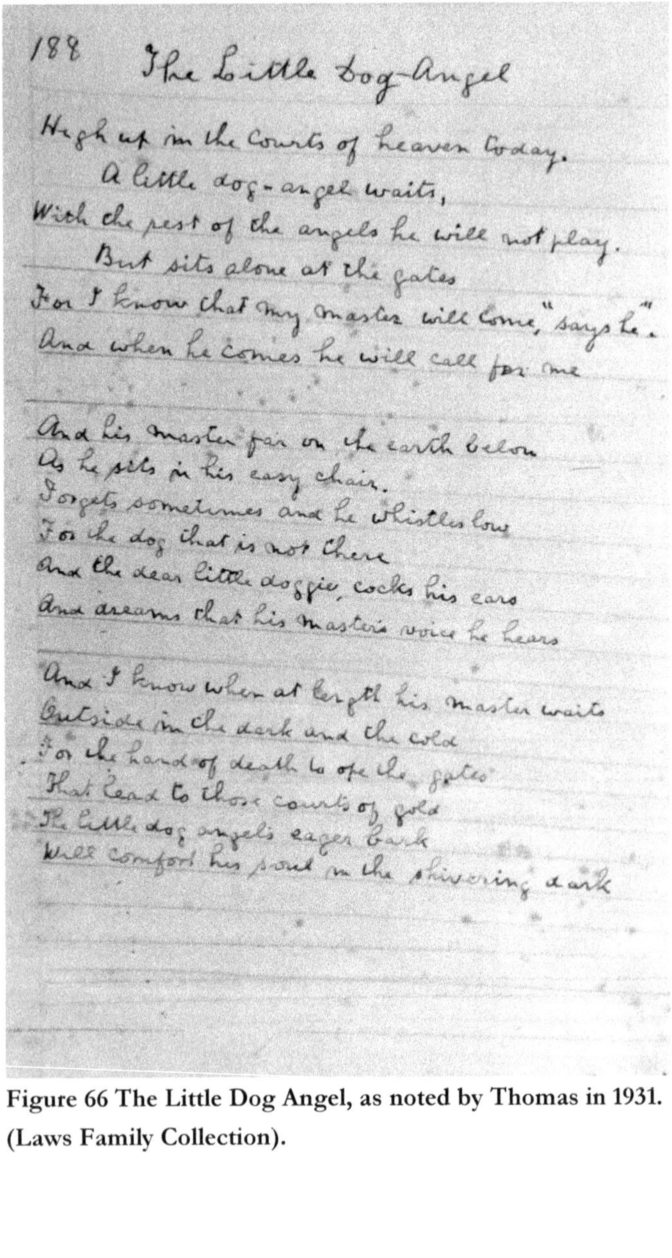

CHAPTER 5

188 **The Little Dog-Angel**

High up in the Courts of heaven today.
    A little dog-angel waits,
With the rest of the angels he will not play.
    But sits alone at the gates
"For I know that my master will come," says he.
"And when he comes he will call for me"

And his master far on the earth below
As he sits in his easy chair.
Forgets sometimes and he whistles low
For the dog that is not there
And the dear little doggie cocks his ears
And dreams that his master's voice he hears

And I know when at length his master waits
Outside in the dark and the cold
For the hand of death to ope the gates
That lead to those courts of gold
The little dog angel's eager bark
Will comfort his soul in the shivering dark

Figure 66 The Little Dog Angel, as noted by Thomas in 1931.
(Laws Family Collection).

Appendix 1: Smallpox and the infant deaths

There were six infant deaths during the voyage of the Douglas. Thomas considered that these were due to lack of proper nourishment, but this was denied by the Ship's doctor. The following correspondence was published in the Wellington Independent in the days immediately after the arrival of the *Douglas* in Wellington.

SHIP DOUGLAS
TO THE EDITOR OF THE INDEPENDENT

SIR,—I wish to officially contradict many exaggerated statements that have been made by the Press of New Zealand in connection with the health of the immigrants from the Douglas, now in the quarantine barracks.

It is true that a few days after leaving England two cases of small pox of a very modified character occurred, the patients being children; they were at once sent into the hospital and kept there until the rash had quite disappeared. Ten days or a fortnight afterwards, other children were similarly affected, and they were separated, but the disease continued to spread amongst the children; but owing to the careful manner in which the authorities in England had insisted on vaccination, and the care taken in examining the children on embarking to see that they had been well vaccinated, together with the excellent sanitary arrangements, that the fine space between decks of the Douglas enabled us to carry out, the disease from beginning to end was of the mildest character, and I have no hesitation in stating that all traces of it were fairly stamped out before the end of July. Letters have been received by the immigrants here, from different parts of the colony, in which it seems some mention is made of destroying wearing apparel, &c. Such a step would be quite unnecessary. By way of precaution all boxes that have been opened during the voyage, together with their contents, will be passed through the fumigation house, and clothing afterwards washed in water containing disinfectants. All luggage will be exposed to sulphur fumigation.

The epidemic of scarlatina has also been limited to the married quarters. All the cases have been of a mild form. We are not quite free from it at present, two young children having had the rash developed since coming on the island. Throughout the voyage I consider the general health of the immigrants has been excellent, and on leaving the island I cannot think that any trace whatever of disease of a contagious character can possibly be conveyed by the passengers. The six infants who died on the voyage out were all under twelve months, and died in the tropics from diarrhœa and marasmas.—Yours &c.,

JOHN TUCK,
Surgeon Superintendent
Somes Island, Oct. 2.

Figure 67 From the Wellington Independent, National Library of New Zealand.

TO THE EDITOR OF THE INDEPENDENT

Sir,—Being one of the immigrants on board the ship Douglas (and writing on behalf of the single men, who can all vouch for what I am about to say), I take the liberty of stating a few facts to you in reference to the report spread about of there being small pox and fever on the ship, and hope you will take notice of it, as we think it will go against us in getting employment.

We had six deaths on the voyage, all of them being infants, and which we are of opinion died through want of sufficient nourishment, there being a very scanty allowance served out to them.

As regards the cases of small-pox, we can certainly say that the doctor must have mistaken it for something else, as we only had a few children sick in the early part of the voyage, and they were well again in a few days; and we sincerely trust that the inhabitants of Wellington will not be led astray by this false report, as the small-pox is a fearful disease, and if it broke out on board ship there is no knowing how many deaths would have occurred. But the most remarkable thing is that the grown-up people were so healthy and are now, and we are positive if the authorities were to see us they would say so too. We will not say much about the fever, as it was only a child's complaint, viz., scarlatina, and which only attacked a few children; but these were well again in a short time.

Figure 68 Wellington Independent, National Library of New Zealand. Text continues on the next figure.

We therefore ask you as a great favor to kindly take notice of this letter, which we hope will be the means of liberating us from this desolate island.—I am, &c,
W. TYRRELL.

Somes Island, October 2

P.S.---We may also mention that Capt. Wilson stated distinctly to-day that his opinion is there was no small pox on board, which entirely denies what he said some time ago in the presence of our chief constable (Sellars), *that there was*. This we can't understand. Whether it is the captain working against the doctor, or the doctor is under a delusion, it is difficult to say ; it must be one or the other. However, I will leave it to you to kindly show it up.

Figure 69 From the Wellington Independent October 1873, National Library of New Zealand.

(PER FAVOR WELLINGTON INDEPENDENT.)

To DR TUCK. Sir—In reference to my letter that was published in the WELLINGTON INDEPENDENT of Friday last, I regret having made statements which you consider slanderous. I had no intention of doing so, or so expressing any adverse opinion of your professional skill. The statements in regard to the children dying from insufficient nourishment, I am very sorry I made. Of course being in the single men's compartment, I could form no opinion.

I trust you will accept this explanation as a retractation of my previous letter.—Yours, &c,
W. TYRRELL.

Somes Island, 8th October, 1873.

Figure 70 From the Wellington Independent October 1873, National Library of New Zealand.

Appendix 2: The ships[113]

SS *Douglas*

The Sailing Ship *Douglas* (Figure 7, page 25) was a three-masted, square-rigged sailing ship. She was made of iron and displaced 1,428 tons. She was chartered jointly by Shaw, Savill Company and the New Zealand Shipping Company for carrying immigrants to New Zealand and carried 388 'assisted immigrant' passengers with a further four in cabins. On the return journey she could carry 8,500 bales of wool.

The accommodation was laid out in a manner similar to other immigrant ships; the single men were grouped together in one compartment, then came the married couples and families, and finally there was a 'protected' compartment for the single women. This was designed to help to prevent 'all immoral or indecent acts or conduct, taking liberties or using improper familiarity with the female passengers'.[114] Thomas and his family travelled on her from London to Wellington in 1873.

---

[113] Much of the technical information in this appendix has come from www.ssmaritime.com by Reuben Goossens.

[114] Queen's order in council 7 January 1864, in David Hastings, Over the mountains of the Sea, Life on the Migrant Ships 1870–1885, Auckland University Press, 2006, ISBN 1-86940-375-4.

PS *Luna*

The Paddle Steamer *Luna* (Figure 16, page 81) carried Thomas and his family from Wellington to Napier in 1873. Six months earlier, the *Luna* had been involved in a delicate diplomatic incident in Kawhia Harbour[115].

SS *Warrimoo*

The Steam Ship *Warrimoo* (Figure 19, page 89) was built by Swan & Hunter Ltd. in 1892 and was operated by the Union Steamship Co. of New Zealand Ltd. She displaced 3,628 tons.

This ship had previously achieved fame by finding herself crossing the equator at the position of the international dateline at midnight on the start of new year's day in 1900. This meant she was, for a brief moment, simultaneously in both 19th and 20th centuries and also in both the northern and southern hemispheres.

Thomas travelled on her from Wellington to Sydney in 1901.

---

[115]https://paperspast.natlib.govt.nz/newspapers/NOT1873040 4.2.12

RMS *Ormuz*

The Royal Mail Service steamer *Ormuz* (Figure 20, page 91) was built by Fairfield Shipbuilding and Engineering Co. Ltd. for the Orient Steam Navigation Co. Ltd. and was launched in 1888 and was claimed by her proud owners to be 'the fastest ship in the world'. There were two ships named *Ormuz*; the one Thomas sailed on was the first *Ormuz* (later renamed *Divona*).

Her displacement was 6,031 tons, and she carried 634 passengers of whom 300 were in 'immigrant' class (i.e. steerage). In addition the *Ormuz* had a high capacity, refrigerated hold. Thomas was in a shared cabin in the second class. He travelled on her from Sydney to London in 1901.

SS *Smeaton*

The Steam Tender *Smeaton* (369 tons) was built by William Allsup of Preston in 1883. She was the first vessel of her type to have screw propulsion instead of the usual paddles. Thomas travelled in her from the anchored *Ormuz* to the wharf at Tilbury in 1901.

RMS *Ortona*

The Royal Mail Service steamer *Ortona*[116] (Figure 55, page 228) was built in 1899 by Vickers, Sons & Maxim Ltd. and was owned by the Pacific Steam Navigation Company. Her displacement was 7,945 tons, and she carried 620 passengers of whom 300 were in third class. Thomas travelled on her from London to Sydney in 1901.

SS *Talune*

The Steam Ship *Talune* (Figure 63, page 266) was built in 1890 by Ramage & Ferguson for the Tasmanian Steam Navigation Company. She displaced 2,087 tons and carried 175 passengers.

The *Talune* achieved a notoriety when, in 1918, she carried influenza to Samoa; 22% of the population of Samoa died as a direct result.[117] The *Talune* had sailed from Auckland, where the epidemic was severe, and she had been quarantined when she stopped in Fiji, but in Samoa passengers were allowed to disembark even if they were ill.

Thomas travelled on the *Talune* from Sydney to Wellington in 1901.

---

[116] In 1910 she was renamed *Arcadian*.

[117] https://nzhistory.govt.nz/culture/1918-influenza-pandemic/samoa

Appendix 3: Who's who?

Many of the people in the 1901 family photograph are mentioned in the diary, and it is useful to name them. In the back row, left to right are: Joseph Coulthard (Susannah's son), Monty, Norman, and Con (the three sons of Jack), Fredrick Farmiloe (Sarah's husband), George (Sallie's son), and Helen (Jack's daughter). In the front row, left to right are: Cuthbert Coulthard (Susannah's husband), Sarah (Susannah's daughter), Thomas, Susannah, Jack, Mary (Jack's second wife), Sallie, and Bertie (Sallie's other son).

Figure 71 The family photograph (Robert Laws Collection).

The following list shows how the three editors of this book are descended from the three brothers, Thomas Laws, John William Laws and Robert Christopher Laws.

Thomas Laws (1840–1934)
Florence Maude Mary Cunnold née Laws (1875–1942)
Florence Muriel Powell née Cunnold (1907–1994)
Elaine Muriel Guise Swann née Powell (1938–)
Joanne Maree Jensen née Swann (1963–)

John William 'Jack' Laws (1852–1937)
Robert Montgomery 'Monty' Laws (1879–1932)
Robert Alan Laws (1916–2003)
Robert Montgomery Laws (1954–)

Robert Christopher 'Bob' Laws (1855–1915)
Gordon Cosgrove Laws (1892–1976)
Derek Gordon Laws (1925–)

The following is part of the Laws family tree starting in 1680 and continuing as far as the generation after Thomas Laws. The unique reference number at the start of each entry represents the descent of that person. In each early generation only one child (written in capital letters) is followed to the next generation. The letters *B*, *M,* and *D* mean *birth, marriage, and death.* The family tree was researched primarily by Gordon Cosgrove Laws and his son, Derek Gordon Laws. Children who died in infancy have been ruled through in the text to avoid confusion: their names are typically used again for a subsequent child. People who are in the family photograph are shown in bold.

1 ROBERT LAWS (Hartburn) B? 1680 D 1730
    M 1708 CATHRIN CROSBY (Hartburn) B? 1682 D 1725

Children of Robert Laws (Cathrin Crosby) ?1680–1730
~~1/1 James Laws 1st (Hartburn) B 1709 D 1711 (died in infancy)~~
1/2 John Laws (Hartburn) B 1711 D ?
1/3 James Laws 2nd (Hartburn) B 1713 D 1731
1/4 WILLIAM LAWS (Kirkharle) B 1716 D 1759
    M 1740 ANN McNEAL (Ponteland) B 1716 D 1746
    M 1747 Mary Gee (Ponteland) B 1720 D 1757
    M 1758 Ann Reay (Ponteland) B 1726 D 1759
1/5 Thomas Laws (Kirkharle) B 1718 D? 1775
    M? 1745 (No Record of Marriage)
1/6 George Laws (Krkharle) B 1721 D? 1781
    M 1753 Catherine Kersop (Stamfordham) B? 1727 D 1755
1/7 Jane Laws (Kirkharle) B 1723 D ?

Children of William Laws (Ann McNeal & Mary Gee) 1716–1759
14/1 ROBERT LAWS (Ponteland) B 1743 D? 1800
    M 1770 ISABEL THOMPSON (Ponteland) B 1747 D 1806
14/2 Thomas Laws (Kirkley) B 1745 D? 1800
    M 1769 Mary Turnbull (Starnfordham) B 1743 D? 1790
14/3 George Laws (Milburn) B 1747 D 1748 (died in infancy)
14/4 Elizabeth Laws (Milburn) B 1748 D ? 1805
    M 1782 Alexander Meggee (Ovington) B ? D ?
14/5 William Laws (Ponteland) B 1753 D ?

Children of Robert Laws (Isabel Thompson) 1743–1806
141/1 Isabel Laws 1st (Stamfordham) B 1772 (died in infancy)
141/2 Ann Laws (Stamfordham) B 1773 D? 1825
    M 1793 George Laidler (Ovington) B 1770 D? 1825
141/3 Mary Laws 1st (Stamfordham) B 1775 (died in infancy)
141/4 Robert Laws (Whalton) B 1777 D? 1835
    M 1804 Margaret Can (Hartburn) B 1779 D? 1835
141/5 John Laws (Milburn) B 1779 D? 1812
    (died in the Peninsula War)
141/6 Mary Laws 2nd (Milburn) B 1781 D ?
141/7 Esther Laws (Milburn) B 1783 D? 1835
    M 1807 Joseph Hall (Ponteland) B? 1780 D? 1840
141/8 THOMAS LAWS (Milburn) B 1785 D 1849
    M 1810 MARY DIXON (Newburn) B 1784 D 1855
141/9 Hannah Laws (Milburn) B 1788 D 1812
141/(10) Sarah Laws (Heddon) B 1791 D 1873
    (The 'Mrs Yeaman' who brought up Thomas at the Seven Stars)
    M? 1815 William Yeaman (Ponteland) B 1786 D 1842
141/(11) William Laws (Milburn) B 1794 D 1850
    M? 1820 Elizabeth Wilkinson B? 1795 D? 1850
141/(12) Isabell Laws 2nd B 1798 D 1799 (drowned in infancy)

Children of Thomas Laws (Mary Dixon) 1785–1849
1418/1 Isabel Laws (Mitford) B 1811 D? 1865
   M 1836 Nicolas Stokoe B? 1810 D? 1870
1418/2 Mary Laws (Milburn Grange) B 1813 D? 1870
   M? 1840 Thomas Hewitt B? 1812 D? 1870
1418/3 ROBERT LAWS (Milburn Grange) B 1815 D 1885
   M 1839 SARAH HOBSON (Morpeth) B 1814 D 1891
1418/4 Thomas Laws (Black Heddon) B 1818 D 1840
   (No Record of Marriage, One Possible Child)
1418/5 Sarah Laws (Milburn Grange) B 1821 D? 1875
   M? 1845 Jonothan Watson B? 1818 D? 1875
1418/6 John Dixon Laws (Milburn Grange) B 1823 D 1871
   M? 1850 Elizabeth Fletcher (Ponteland) B? 1826 D 1906
1418/7 William Laws (Milburn Grange) B 1825 D 1903
   M? 1852 Ann Oliver B? 1826 D? 1881

Children of Robert Laws (Sarah Hobson) 1815–1885
14183/1 Thomas Laws (Ponteland) B 1840 D 1934
   M 1865 Mary Ann 'Polly' Newlands (Newcastle) B 1842 D 1919
   (Emigrated to Napier, New Zealand, on SS *Douglas* in 1873)
~~14183/2 Susannah Laws 1st (Ponteland) B 1842 D 1846 (died aged 3½)~~
14183/3 Mary Laws (Ponteland) B 1845 D 1891 (Never Married)
14183/4 Sarah Yeaman 'Sallie' Laws (Ponteland) B 1847 D 1936
   M 1875 George Robert Dodds (Newcastle) B 1847 D 1901
14183/5 Susannah Laws 2nd (Ponteland) B 1849 D 1903
   M 1876 Cuthbert Coulthard (Garnigills) B 1846 D 1911
14183/6 John William 'Jack' Laws (Ponteland) B 1852 D 1937
   M 1876 Barbara Shanks Richardson (Newcastle) B 1851 D 1887
   M 1889 Mary Dickenson (Cox Green) B 1857 D 1942
14183/7 Elizabeth Jane 'Lil' Laws (Ponteland) B 1854 D 1911
   M 1876 John James Bollard (Newcastle) B 1854 D 1882
   M 1890 James Thompson (Newcastle) B 1860 D 1936
14183/8 Robert Christopher 'Bob' Laws (Ponteland) B 1855 D 1915
   M 1877 Isabella Cullen (Murton Colliery) B 1859 D 1931
   (Emigrated to Napier, New Zealand, on SS *Rakaia* in 1879)

Children of Thomas Laws (Mary Ann 'Polly' Newlands) 1840–1931
(Emigrated to Napier, New Zealand on SS *Douglas* 1873)
141831/1 Charles Henry Laws B 1867 D 1958
   M 1892 Charlotte Emily England (Sis) B 1867 D 1946
~~141831/2 William Yeaman 'Willie' Laws B 1869 D 1869 (died in infancy)~~
141831/3 Frederick Arthur Laws B 1871 D 1954
   M 1902 Amelia Trevor B 1874 D 1934
14183/4 Florence Maude Mary Laws B 1875 D 1942
   M 1897 Charles George Cunnold B 1867 D 1949
14183/5 Evelyn Lucy Laws B 1877 D 1961 (Never Married)
14183/6 Edwin Vincent Laws B 1879 D 1949
   M 1903 Isabella Agnes Vincent B 1876 D 1919
   M 1926 Grace Dorothy Horsley B 1891 D 1991
14183/7 Mabel Chancellor Laws B 1885 D 1965
   M 1907 Edward Mulinder B 1883 D 1909
   M 1916 Martin Joseph Lenihan (Joseph) B 1876 D 1966
14183/8 Bertha Gertrude Laws B 1886 D 1972
   M 1915 Frank Mairs B 1889 D 1965

Children of Sarah Yeaman Laws (George Dodds) 1847–1936)
141834/1 George Robert Dodds B 1876 D 1946
   M 1907 Agnes Winter B? 1882 D 1944 (No Children)
141834/2 Herbert Yeaman 'Bert' Dodds B 1878 D 1941
   M 1908 Violet Katherine Bewick B 1884 D 1929
   M 1931 Frances Mary Chapman B 1905 D 1996
   (Mary Subsequently Re-Married)
~~141834/3 Sidney Colverwell Dodds B 1880 D 1881 (died in infancy)~~

Children of Susannah Laws 2nd (Cuthbert Coulthard) 1849–1903
141835/1 Sarah Frances Coulthard B 1877 D 1964
   M 1898 Frederick Farmiloe (No Children) B 1871 D 1964
141835/2 Joseph Coulthard B 1880 D 1959
   M 1909 Minniem Stokoe B1881 D 1956

Children of John William Laws (Barbara Shanks Richardson) 1852–1937
~~141836/1 Robert Montgomery Laws 1st B 1877 D 1878 (died in infancy)~~
~~141836/2 Helen Laws 1st B 1878 D 1878 (died in infancy)~~
141836/3 Robert Montgomery 'Monty' Laws 2nd B 1879 D 1932
  M 1913 Lucy Ellen Ibbotson B 1886 D 1968
141836/4 John William Coningsby 'Con' Laws B 1881 D 1957
  M 1907 Anne Dobson B ? D 1951
141836/5 Helen 'Nenna' Laws 2nd B 1883 D 1972
  M 1905 Joseph Ostens B 1874 D 1940
141836/6 Norman Stuart Vivian Laws B 1885 D 1954
  M 1912 Emma Jane Swaddle B 1882 D 1968

Children of Elizabeth Jane Laws (John James Bolland) 1854–1911
141837/1 Florence Jane Joice Bolland B 1877 D 1957 (Never Married)
141837/2 Edith Susannah Bolland B 1878 D 1960 (Never Married)
141837/3 John Burton Bolland B 1880 D ?

Children of Robert Christopher Laws (Isabella Cullen) 1855–1915)
(Emigrated to Napier, New Zealand on SS *Rakaia* 1879)
141838/1 Elizabeth Simpson 'Liz' Laws B 1878 D 1956
    M 1908 Christopher John Coppin (No Children) B 1876 D 1940
141838/2 Sarah Hobson Laws B 1880 D 1951
    M 1904 Joseph Clark B 1866 D 1965
141838/3 Henrietta Mary 'Het' Laws B 1881 D 1958
    M 1907 Alfred Francis Kirk B 1881 D 1953
141838/4 Robert 'Bob' Laws B 1883 D 1956
    M 1913 Esther Whyte Diggle B 1891 D 1957
141838/5 Ethel Vivienne Isobel Laws B 1884 D 1918
    M 1908 Albert John Harvey (ReM 1926) B 1881 D 1961
141838/6 Ruth Ivy Laws B 1888 D 1972
    M 1918 Arthur Hilson Ramlose B 1883 D 1948
141838/7 Hubert Victor 'Buck' Laws B 1890 D 1967
    M 1928 Helena Josephine Jarman (No Children)B 1886 D 1956
141838/8 Gordon Cosgrove Laws B 1892 D 1976
    M 1916 Jane Willis 'Jean' Russell B 1894 D 1979
141838/9 Hector Percy Charlton Laws B 1894 D 1916
    (Killed In Action, France WW1)
141838/(10) Christina Clark 'Chrissy' Laws B 1896 D 1926
    M 1924 William James Pratley (later re-married) B 1900 D 1980
141838/(11) Thomas 'Tom' or 'Buck' Laws B 1901 D 1975
    M 1928 Loma McCormick B 1908 D 1976
141838/(12) John William 'Jack' Laws (another one) B 1903 D 1994
    M 1928 Laura Anne Johncock B 1905 D 1990

CPSIA information can be obtained
at www.ICGtesting.com
Printed in the USA
BVHW07s0820221018
530873BV00001B/31/P

9 781388 192259